LAUGHING ALL THE WAY

KAREN O'CONNOR

HARVEST HOUSE PUBLISHERS
EUGENE, OREGON

Cover design and illustration by Dugan Design Group

Published in association with Books & Such Management, 52 Mission Circle, Suite 122, PMB 170, Santa Rosa, CA 95409-5370, www.booksandsuch.com.

Names and details have been changed to protect individuals' identity.

LAUGHING ALL THE WAY
Copyright © 2018 by Karen O'Connor
Published by Harvest House Publishers
Eugene, Oregon 97408
www.harvesthousepublishers.com

ISBN 978-0-7369-7364-9 (pbk.)
ISBN 978-0-7369-7365-6 (eBook)

Library of Congress Cataloging-in-Publication Data

Names: O'Connor, Karen, author.
Title: Laughing all the way / Karen O'Connor.
Description: Eugene : Harvest House Publishers, 2018.
Identifiers: LCCN 2017061381 (print) | LCCN 2018013878 (ebook) | ISBN
    9780736973656 (ebook) | ISBN 9780736973649 (pbk.)
Subjects: LCSH: Aging—Religious aspects—Christianity. | Older
    people—Religious life. | Laughter—Religious aspects—Christianity.
Classification: LCC BV4580 (ebook) | LCC BV4580 .O366 2018 (print) | DDC
    248.8/5—dc23
LC record available at https://lccn.loc.gov/2017061381

Printed in the United States of America

21 22 23 24 25 26 / VP-GL / 10 9 8 7 6

For June, my sister and best friend

RIP

. . . .

For Carol Sue, a silver-and-gold friend

Contents

Part One

Making New Choices

Part Two

Accepting New Challenges

Part Three

Taking New Chances

Part Four

Opening New Chapters

Up for New Opportunities?

"The tragedy of life is not that it ends too soon, but that we wait so long to begin it," said William Mather Lewis, an American teacher, university president, and government official. This quote gave me pause as I considered my life now that I'm heading down the home stretch. Do I give up and just watch TV or do I open the door and walk outside eager for what God might bring my way today? I want to open the door, but sometimes I'm afraid or worried or anxious about what might be out there. Now that I'm a widow and living alone, I realize how much I relied on my partnership with my husband. We made decisions together. We traveled together. We talked with one another. We figured things out side by side.

You may have similar concerns as you look ahead. So I've divided this book into four sections, each one focusing on some of the *new* opportunities that come our way as we step into the golden years, which at times may look and feel more like tarnished silver.

- *Making New Choices* will cover some of the ways we can become involved with new people and places, as well as new ways of thinking.

- *Accepting New Challenges* will highlight the inevitable experiences that are part of the aging process, such as illnesses, losses, and possible financial worries. We'll look at how we can accept and work with them in positive ways—and even smile through them.

- *Taking New Chances* will prompt us to risk more and worry less, to do that thing we've always wanted to do—whether it's taking singing lessons, or running a marathon, or repairing a broken friendship.

- *Opening New Chapters* will suggest ways to rekindle your relationship with God, keys to living in the heartland of gratitude and joy regardless of the circumstances, and the markers to help you realize that growing old is truly a "privilege few people get to experience."

Above all, God is with us. Proverbs 3:5-6 (MSG) says:

> Trust God from the bottom of your heart; don't try to figure out everything on your own. Listen for God's voice in everything you do, everywhere you go; he's the one who will keep you on track. Don't assume that you know it all. Run to God! Run from evil! Your body will glow with health, your very bones will vibrate with life! Honor God with everything you own; give him the first and the best. Your barns will burst, your wine vats will brim over. But don't, dear friend, resent God's discipline; don't sulk under his loving correction. It's the child he loves that God corrects; a father's delight is behind all this.

I hope you will carry this message from God as well as the practical examples in this book to others who are traveling with you and those who will soon join you on this journey to heaven—and most of all that you'll laugh—or at least smile—and trust all the way. I'm walking this road with you.

Karen O'Connor

Part One

Making New Choices

Choice: An act of selecting or making a decision
when faced with two or more possibilities:
the choice between good and evil.

NEW OXFORD AMERICAN DICTIONARY

. . . .

Birds of a Feather

Birds of a feather flock together,
And so will pigs and swine;
Rats and mice will have their choice,
And so will I have mine.

NURSERY RHYME

I laughed out loud when I stumbled on this old Mother Goose
nursery rhyme while preparing a writing class for young students.
It reminded me that I always have a *choice*. I'm not held captive to
the opinions or choices of others, which is so important to remember—especially during our golden years. Let's look at making some
choices, resisting temptation when it comes to personal desires,
sharing ourselves with others, and dealing with past hurts.

1

What's So Funny About Getting Old-er?

Making a Choice to Enjoy Aging

What's so humorous about aging? Some older folks might respond, "Not much." And then they launch into their list of aches and pains, valid as they might be. On the other hand, there is plenty to chuckle about—misplacing our glasses, or hearing aids, or cell phones, for example—because when we get right down to it, *life* can be funny at any age. We just need to be willing to look for the sweet surprises, little jokes, and unexpected oopsies that make us laugh out loud.

Martin Luther, father of the Reformation movement and a theologian, made no bones about the funny side of life. "If I'm not allowed to laugh in heaven, then I don't want to go there," he said. American theologian Reinhold Niebuhr went so far as to say, "Humor is, in fact, a prelude to faith, and laughter is the beginning of prayer." I love that one! "A prelude to faith" and "the beginning of prayer." What a beautiful perspective. With that thought in mind we need never be worried or embarrassed to smile at life and even laugh about it. When the elders of Charles Spurgeon's church asked him to tone down his humor in the pulpit, the famous minister was quick to respond: "Gentlemen, if you only knew how much I held back!"

I'm thinking life would be pretty challenging if we didn't stop and let out a good belly laugh once in a while—even several times a day. Many great preachers and writers knew this and practiced it in their own lives despite the sadness and evil in the world around them.

Oh, Lord! Here Comes Another Senior Moment

When I tumbled into my sixties, all of a sudden there they were—those dreaded senior moments I'd noticed in my parents and relatives when they became seniors. Lost keys, unpaid bills, missed medical appointments, and a pair of socks on my husband's workbench instead of in his dresser drawer. I could join in with others and hope they'd laugh with me—even though sometimes I was too embarrassed to admit my mishaps.

I decided to step out instead of hiding out—and write about them. So I wrote a book for people like me—the over-fifty crowd, hoping they would enjoy a good laugh and a sigh of relief that they were not alone. A few years after Harvest House published my book *Gettin' Old Ain't for Wimps*, I received a note from a loyal reader letting me know that my funny stories and Bible quotes were the focus of that year's women's Bible study in her church. What a surprise! Did she really want to pass off my book as a serious Scripture study?

"The ladies and I read one story a week and have a good laugh over our morning coffee and pastry," she said. Later they read the Bible verse included and talked about how it applies to their lives. "It's the best Bible study we've ever done."

What a joy to find out that a book I'd intended for entertainment and a brief spiritual moment became a source of spiritual nourishment for a group of senior women like me.

I was happy that others agreed that we all need a dose of laughter and joy on a daily basis. As seniors, we can choose to focus on the hurts and disappointments, or we can turn the lens of perspective and see them as opportunities to trust God, share encouraging words with others, and resolve problems while at the same time looking for the *new* lessons we can discover. God reminds us in John 10:10: "I have come that they may have life, and have it to the full."

Oh, No—Not That!

"Guess what?" The expression on my husband's face as he stood in the doorway alerted me that something was wrong. "I washed my pants with my wallet still in the back pocket," he said, his face wrinkled with shame. He held up his soggy billfold and its contents, drops of water hitting the floor. How could he be so absentminded? But then we burst out laughing. Yep! This man was up to no good. *He pleaded guilty to laundering our money!*

Hmmm! A perfect anecdote for one of my books, I decided. After that, we agreed that Charles would supply the senior moments, I'd do the writing, and we'd share the income. Perfection.

Life and Laughter

You don't have to be a stand-up comedian to entertain your friends and yourself and generate good belly laughs. When my sister died last year, I offered to deliver one of the eulogies for our family. I knew it would be a somber occasion, and I didn't want to add to the sadness. I tucked in a few funny experiences about our relationship to bring smiles to those who had come to honor her life and memory.

"June and I shared many things—friendship, paper dolls, board games—*and* measles, mumps, chicken pox, and scarlet fever." These were small details, but they caught people by surprise, and they roared with laughter. I added a few more humorous episodes and then closed with a beautiful quote from *The Imitation of Christ* by Thomas á Kempis, an author my sister and I admired and respected.

One of the things I've learned as a writer of humor and inspiration is that blending the two makes each a little sweeter and certainly appeals to us because it sounds more human.

My friend Melissa supplied me with a few chuckles when she called to tell me she sprayed her hair with furniture polish by mistake. "It fell flat but had a nice sheen!" she said. Hooray for seniors! We can laugh together at the silly stuff we mistakenly do.

I'm not without a few of my own senior moments. I once thought I'd misplaced my cell phone only to discover I was using it right then to speak with my neighbor. *Oh my!*

Movies and Mayhem

My son loves funny movies. So when he visits during the Christmas holidays, we all watch *What About Bob* with Bill Murray and *Elf* with Will Ferrell. It feels good to sit around munching snacks and giggling over the ridiculous banter and over-the-top humor.

A woman whose hair was growing in after chemo treatments said her husband helped her laugh about a situation that was definitely hard to face in public. "Now we can save a few bucks. No more weekly trips to the hairdresser," he quipped when the moment was right.

Humor in the Bible

The Bible refers to joy and laughter. Here are a few verses I like to turn to when I'm feeling pressure or anxiety—even over small things that crop up during the day:

- "Our mouths were filled with laughter, our tongues with songs of joy" (Psalm 126:2).
- "A happy heart makes the face cheerful" (Proverbs 15:13).
- "A cheerful heart is good medicine" (Proverbs 17:22).
- "Blessed are you who weep now, for you will laugh" (Luke 6:21).

A Happy Heart

Did you know that blood flow increases and blood vessels function better when you laugh, resulting in protection against a heart attack and other cardiovascular problems? "Your sense of humor is one of the most powerful tools you have to make certain that your daily mood and emotional state support good health," says Paul E. McGhee, PhD, a pioneer in humor research. American clergyman and activist Henry Ward Beecher once said, "Mirth is God's best medicine. Everybody ought to bathe in it."

Voltaire, a French philosopher and author, put humor and health into perspective during the seventeenth century: "The art of medicine consists of keeping the patient amused while nature heals the disease." The late comedienne Phyllis Diller, at age 93, said, "Laughter fluffs up every cell in your body." Hooray for fluffy cells as we grow older!

I attribute my good health and that of some of the healthiest people I know to being able to enjoy a good laugh, especially at our own expense. Living under a cloud of worry pulls us down. Smiling in the sunshine of life keeps us going and doing and giving to others. I'm for that. How about you? We can be ambassadors of help and humor, and we'll enjoy the benefits in our own lives.

Spiritual Health

Humor also helps us hold on to a positive, optimistic outlook during times of trouble. Even a small smile can turn things around at least momentarily, and give us a new perspective...maybe even a solution. Look to Jesus for joy. He delighted in little children, enjoyed walking and communing with his followers, and reminded Martha to take a tip from her sister, Mary, who chose relationship over duty (at least some of the time).

Looking at our lives in perspective can release our lighter side, help us connect with our inner child, and rely more on our God of love to help us release our senior moments with hearty chuckles. Let's choose to find the fun and humor in aging.

. . . .

Wit:

"I never made a mistake in my life. I thought I did once, but I was wrong." CHARLES M. SCHULZ

Wisdom:

"We all stumble in many ways" (James 3:2).

Willpower:

"I will count myself human and be okay with my senior moments. After all, I am a senior."

2

When You Feel like Making a U-Turn

Making a Choice to Move Forward

These beautiful Bible verses hold wisdom for the ages—especially as we grow older. When I think of some of the decisions I made in the past, I shudder. Was I worthy of such grace and forgiveness? But Jesus tells us it's not about being *worthy*. Our behavior doesn't merit God's favor. He loves us. Period. *Whew!*

Do you want to turn away from your past too? If only we could flip a switch, and the darkness would disappear forever. On the other hand, how comforting to know that when we come to God in our weakness he embraces us. As we would our own children, he not only forgives, he forgets.

> *As far as the east is from the west, so far has he removed our transgressions from us.*
>
> PSALM 103:12

Shame and Blame

"Shame" and "Blame" are two "siblings" who can't seem to live without one another. Blame causes Shame and Shame resorts to Blame in order to survive. I couldn't get past my past until I realized through prayer, counseling, and meditating on God's promises that when I hold on to what God has already let go of, I'm tossing out his grace as if it were the daily trash.

On the first day after I decided to follow Jesus Christ as my Lord, I made a new resolution. I wasn't looking to try a new diet, or join a gym, or read the Bible from cover to cover. No, I decided to *let go of my past*, to give up the part of my life I was ashamed of. I stopped dwelling on the fact that I was divorced. That for a time I lived apart from two of my children. That I lacked the fortitude to drop a friend who was disrupting my life. And on and on my list went. I wrote down every shameful action or situation I could think of. And then I tore it up. I didn't even reread it. I was finished with Blame and Shame. I gave them the boot.

Of course, regrets came up from time to time. A wayward thought tried to intrude on a peaceful day, but right then and there I stopped it in its tracks. I turned to one of my favorite Bible verses and calmed down.

Know therefore that the LORD your God is God; he is the faithful God, keeping his covenant of love to a thousand generations of those who love him and keep his commandments.
DEUTERONOMY 7:9

God is faithful. He doesn't measure his love and grace by what we do or don't do. He loves *everyone* because *God is love.* John Wesley reminded his congregation that an experience of the divine is always "a warming of the heart." That warming is an experience every bit as tangible as enjoying a fresh croissant with butter and jam or a little child crawling into your lap and saying, "I love you."

God is *never* about blame, shame, and guilt. *Never!* He is the perfect parent, friend, brother, and Lord. He takes on the responsibility and the consequences of our actions *for* each of us. We are free because of his love.

So what became of those shameful experiences in my life? How did God redeem them?

- Ending my marriage after my husband left our family led me to Christ, the only one who really knew my pain and sorrow.

- Living apart from two of my children for a time gave me the opportunity to grow up and become the mother they needed and deserved.

- Facing a harmful relationship head-on helped me to speak up for myself and to trust God for what I needed.

Every area of my past that hung over me God transformed into a gift of grace.

A New Point of View

A woman I met a few years ago told me about an experience she had with her father who had heaped abuse on her as a child. Her personal story sent chills up my spine. Her dad had never expressed any love for her—only disappointment that she wasn't the son he'd longed for. His high standards for her in school and in sports kept her anxious and worried, knowing that when she missed the mark he'd punish her with the silent treatment for days at a time.

"I grew up with a cloud of doubt hanging over me until I was married and became a mother," Sheila said. "I never wanted to do to my kids what my father had done to me."

Although Sheila knew God loved her, she couldn't let go of the longing to hear her human father say "I love you" at least once to her. One day, after years of separation, her mother phoned to say Sheila's dad was in the hospital following a stroke. Sheila flew across the country and hurried to his hospital room. "I stood for a moment in the doorway," she said, "surprised by the small, frail body nestled in the center of the bed, his head resting on a pillow that seemed too big. 'He's just an old and frail man now,' I thought. 'No longer the big guy that I was terrified of displeasing.'" Tears spilled down her cheeks. "All I wanted to do was kiss my dad and tell him I loved him. It didn't matter whether he said the same to me. I was 62 years old. He was 89. It was time to let go of the past." Sheila reached for her father's hand, whispered her love for him, and thanked him for giving her life.

He squeezed her hand and whispered, "I'm glad I had a daughter after all. I love you."

Sheila could barely speak. She kissed her father on his forehead. "In that moment, every bitter thought I'd held against him vanished," she said. "God is faithful to the end."

Letting Go

There comes a time when we must let go of our past so we can live in the present and face the future. Why not do it today? Tomorrow might be too late. God has us in his grip and will never turn away from us—no matter what other people do to us or what we do to ourselves. Choosing to let go of the past is something to smile about—and maybe even turn into a good laugh! Without our God, we are helpless, but *with him all things are possible.*

. . . .

Wit:

"To thrive in life you need three bones: a wishbone, a backbone, and a funny bone." REBA MCENTIRE

Wisdom:

"Forget the former things; do not dwell on the past. See, I am doing a new thing!" (Isaiah 43:18-19).

Willpower:

"Instead of looking back, today I will look forward."

3

From Desperation to Inspiration—Heidi's Story

Making a Choice to Turn from Addictions

My friend Heidi slipped a hand into her pants pocket and pulled out a small square of paper with the number 4,857 written on it. Anyone who does not know Heidi's amazing story might frown in puzzlement. What do the paper and number mean? They signify how many days she's been sober after many years of alcohol addiction.

Heidi's husband, Dick, supports her in this unique way. Each morning he writes down a new number on a fresh square of paper and has it ready for Heidi to pick up at the breakfast table. She tucks it into her pocket for the next 24 hours until it's time to trade it in for the new number.

As of this writing she has achieved more than 4,857 days of recovery. She's also written three short inspirational books illustrated with her own photographs that tell her story and inspire others to share theirs.

I'm eager for you to get to know her too. Heidi is not shy or embarrassed to share her journey. Being open has transformed her life and led to profound changes in the lives of everyone who knows her.

"I'm an alcoholic in recovery," Heidi is quick to admit. "I got sober three days before my fiftieth birthday (she is now 63). I'd been trying to get there for many years." Not until she surrendered to God completely was she able to stop drinking for good.

"I didn't start out to write a book. I was just jotting down the many daily thoughts from God and friends that crossed my mind on how to stay sober. One day I had so many thoughts, I started compiling them into short one-page writings with photos."

The first book was born: *Free Beer Tomorrow.* Then *Hair of the Dog*, and finally, *I'll Have Mine Straight Up.* (For more information, see www.SquareBooksintheLight.com.)

Heidi said the books almost wrote themselves as she listened to God speak to her heart. "I just know I was compelled to write." Her books deal with alcohol addiction, and they're for people who have a hard time believing in what Alcoholics Anonymous refers to as one's "higher power."

According to Heidi, "All three books provide a 'soft landing' into the concept of depending on God—the power greater than ourselves—for help. The books are short messages about the journey from desperation to inspiration." From her own experiences, Heidi encourages others: "Never give up hope for yourself or your loved ones. If I can remain sober so can you."

On the Rise

"Drug and alcohol abuse among the elderly is a rapidly growing health problem in the United States," according to Richard A. Friedman, MD, of NYTimes.com, as quoted on the Addiction Center website. And the effects can be devastating due to declining health in later years. Older men and women often give in to feelings of uselessness during retirement, or sadness and loneliness following the death of a spouse or other loved one.

Surrendering to God is key, claims Heidi. Then going to meetings and, ultimately, serving others. "You don't have to do this alone. In fact, you can't do it alone." Heidi also reminds addicts of any kind that their addiction is not who they are at their core. "You can rise above it," she adds.

So many people helped Heidi when she started her journey to sober living that she now wants to give back by encouraging and serving others. "It has been an unbelievable journey to hear from people how my books have impacted them or have been used as tools to tip somebody over to the side of getting into recovery. It keeps me sober knowing I stand in the gap for others through prayer and through my books. I think of it as a form of service."

If you or someone you know is suffering from addiction of any kind—drugs, alcohol, pain medication, relationship dependency, overeating—help is available. A good place to start is with Heidi's books.

> No personal calamity is so
> crushing that something true and
> great can't be made of it.
>
> BILL W., ALCOHOLICS ANONYMOUS FOUNDER

Now there's something to smile about, so let's get on with making something true and great out of our personal addictions—now.

. . . .

Wit:

"We all have baggage; find someone who loves you enough to help you unpack." AUTHOR UNKNOWN

Wisdom:

"The eternal God is your refuge, and underneath are the everlasting arms" (Deuteronomy 33:27).

Willpower:

"I will live my life one day at a time. The past is over; the future is yet to be."

4

Fruitful Giving

Making a Choice to Share Ourselves

A couple of years ago I signed up for a hike with a group of seniors.
We were to gather at a certain location and go from there. I left home
early because I wasn't sure of the meeting place and didn't want to be
late, so I arrived about 15 minutes ahead of time. I noticed a woman
standing alone on the corner near where I'd parked. She was wearing a daypack and hiking shoes, so I assumed she was there for the
same purpose I was.

I approached her, introduced myself, and she gave me her name.
We discovered we were both single, had Irish heritage, and lived in
the same neighborhood. That gave us plenty to talk about. I knew
I had just made a new friend. She loved movies, so we agreed to get
together for a film and a meal in the next week or two.

What started that day has led to more than two years of mutual
"fruitful giving." We enjoy each other's company, and we try to stay
current with films that come to the art theater in our town. The
best part of our growing friendship is that, from the day we met,

we've been able to move forward. We didn't need to fill each other in on our entire life history. Once we were strangers, and now we are good friends.

Not a Stranger Among Us

There are many ways to give to people. At a recent church meeting a group of us were talking about the homeless population in our city and wondering how we could help. Men and women alone or with children and babies stand at busy intersections or near the stores in a mall holding signs and begging for food or money. We agreed that a few dollars on the spot doesn't really help in the long run. With that, one of the women pulled out sheets of information she'd found on the Internet. They listed resources in our area that are free of charge for those in need, including showers, food, and shelter. We each took one. I made copies at home and keep them in my car so I can pass it to someone in obvious need. It's a small gesture, but it's at least one thing I can do.

Spontaneous Fruit!

One February, Charles bought a package of valentines, one for each of our grandchildren. After signing his name and filling out the envelopes, he joined a long line at the post office to buy stamps. It was a warm day, and there were too few clerks behind the counter. As he thumbed through the valentines one last time, he realized he had a spare one. Angela was the clerk who would serve him. She looked harried and weary as she scanned the crowd of customers. Quickly Charles scribbled her name across the blank envelope, signed his name to the card, and stepped up to her window. He asked for a book of stamps, laid a $20 bill on the counter, took his change, and slid the spare valentine marked "Angela" across the counter. "Have a happy one," he said and then disappeared out the door.

Charles hoped his gesture brought a smile to Angela's face. What he didn't expect was how happy *he* felt! "Such a small thing," he mused, "and such a big feeling."

What a great example of how one moment in time—like a breeze on a lake—can create a ripple that lasts for hours, perhaps days, even months, all because one person did on the spot what his heart led him to do.

Such moments are there for each one of us if we're alert and ready to act on them. How about buying two concert tickets and inviting a friend—your treat? Or filling an extra grocery bag with some bread and cheese and fruit and dropping it off at a rescue mission? You can hold the door for the man or woman behind you. Meet and greet someone who appears shy or awkward. Do a load of laundry, or mow the lawn, or empty the dishwasher even if it's not your job or your day to do it. What you do in secret for the Father, your heavenly Father will reward. These are ideas to consider—not things to force or even necessarily to plan. Opportunities pop up like sunflowers in summer.

I'm now substitute teaching one or two days a week at a private Christian school in my community. I didn't expect to love it as much as I do. The youthful energy, the beautiful campus, the values taught there all contribute joy to my life in ways I never expected. And I'm earning a bit of pocket money too—so all is well. As I share my fruit with the students and teachers, they share theirs with me.

Jesus was the perfect example of fruitful giving. He laid his loving, healing hands on people—holding children on his knee, sharing a kiss of greeting, embracing his mother and the disciples. His loving touch, as well as his words said in love, drew people to him.

Surely we can do the same in our own way and walk away with a big smile on our face.

．．．．．．．．．．．

Wit:

"A mind is like a parachute. It doesn't work if it is not open." FRANK ZAPPA

Wisdom:

"Give, and it will be given to you. A good measure, pressed down, shaken together and running over, will be poured into your lap" (Luke 6:38).

Willpower:

"I will set aside my snap judgments today and be open to being with others as opportunities present themselves."

5

Comforting the Comfortless

Making a Choice to Serve in a New Way

Years ago as a new Christian, I was all about serving. I received much advice and many suggestions for how I could minister to others. Pass the basket at church, collect food for the homeless, donate clothing and toys for orphans in Mexico, deliver food for new moms and church members recovering from hospital stays, and so much more.

"Hmm. Where do I fit?" I wondered aloud. After much thought I decided to join the Kitchen Angels and prepare a meal once or twice a month, as needed, for those who were housebound for a time. I liked to cook and I enjoyed the idea of preparing full-course meals for others. I could already envision their smiling faces when I came to the door with a dinner that was ready to serve within minutes.

The first week I was very excited as I thumbed through my cookbooks looking for the perfect meal that would be a hit with anyone I was assigned to help. I settled on chicken parmesan, a favorite with most folks. And to that I added a mixed green salad, bread sticks, whipped potatoes, and a yummy chocolate concoction for dessert. I included a bottle of chilled apple cider, colorful paper napkins, disposable cups, plates, and utensils. I had this dialed in.

I delivered the feast to a family close to my home, and they were delighted and grateful. I was off and running. Within weeks my run slowed to a limp. My meals became simpler and simpler until they were reduced to deli sandwiches, chips, ice cream and cookies—all of which I could assemble in a matter of minutes. Good thing because some of the people I was to serve lived across town, which meant facing late-afternoon traffic on congested streets.

Before long my angel wings fell off and there was no retrieving them. I was simply not cut out for this kind of service, and the committee head saw it before I did. She let me go gently—or did she fire me? I'm not sure. I felt dreadful about what I considered a failure.

A Hefty Dose of Grace

As I grew in my spiritual life, I realized that serving others doesn't necessarily mean *sacrifice* to the point of self-depletion. In other words, I didn't have to wring every ounce of strength from my mind and body to be of use to someone in need. *In fact,* I wondered, *what does it mean to serve, anyway?* I'm pretty sure as I look back on that period of my life, I thought it had to be a kind of penalty or it didn't count. It had to hurt or be unpleasant. It never occurred to me then that serving others can and should come from a place of joy and generosity—like Brother Lawrence, the seventeenth-century friar who took pleasure in sweeping the floor of the kitchen monastery where he was assigned to do his part. He once said that he found God in the kitchen more than he ever did in the chapel.

Over the years since my misplaced first attempt at serving others, I have discovered through reading and by experience that for *me* the best service I can offer is *comfort,* doing what I can to help alleviate someone's grief or distress, whether in the moment or over time.

Sometimes offering comfort is simply *sitting* with someone, listening, and then praying aloud or in silence for God to touch that person's spirit with his gentle love and kindness, the type of comfort he gave me on my worst days.

As a writer, teacher, and speaker, I deal with words, words, and more words on a daily basis. It has been a lesson in humility and patience to serve up *in* silence a heaping helping of comfort that does not require verbal output. I'm also learning that people usually have the necessary resources within themselves to make new choices that can lead to brave decisions when someone who cares simply sits alongside them in support as they process their worry, or pain, or grief, or confusion.

A woman named Fran did that for me when I was young and inexperienced and too full of words for others, whether they asked for them or not. Fran helped me to calm down, to let go of the "shoulds" I'd put on myself, and to trust that the God of all comfort would always be there for me.

Of course, now I know that our comforting God, the blessed Holy Spirit, will comfort all who come to him directly or through a loving comforter who notices their pain and sits through it with them.

As I said, I'm not so quick to bake a cake, gather a basket of canned goods, hold a fundraiser, or go on a mission trip, as wise and good as such activities are. I focus on *comforting* others, as God has comforted me.

How do you best serve others? Isn't it nice to know that when you feel good about yourself and those you serve, you are in the center of God's will for you? Doesn't knowing that help you smile and laugh right along with the God of all comfort?

. . . .

Wit:

"Deal with the faults of others as gently as with your own." CHINESE PROVERB

Wisdom:

"Praise be to…the God of all comfort, who comforts us in all our troubles, so that we can comfort those in any trouble with the comfort we ourselves receive from God" (2 Corinthians 1:3-4).

Willpower:

"Today I'm going to offer comfort to those who seem in need—not with advice or over-caretaking but with a smile, or word, or welcoming nod, or maybe just quiet companionship."

6

Set the Table and Invite Some Friends

Making a Choice to Be Hospitable

"I'm done cooking."

"Kitchen's closed."

"Let's eat out."

These are just a few of the exclamations I've overheard from couples and singles who hit their golden years. They don't want to spend the time and the effort with the prep, the mess, and the cleanup. It's easier to meet friends and family at restaurants.

But is it really? On the surface maybe, but after a while you may notice something missing—at least I did. I missed sharing the warmth of my home, the pretty dishes gathering dust in my china cabinet, the silverware needing a good polishing, and the favorite recipes hiding in a file in a kitchen drawer I rarely opened. But most of all I missed the company, the laughter, and the opportunity to share my hospitality with others. So what if it took a little extra time and effort? I'm a senior, but I'm not *that* busy.

Just Do It!

Then came the day. My husband and I sank into our new living room chairs and sipped a glass of iced tea as we admired the freshly painted walls, the polished tables, and a lovely new painting hanging above the sofa. The living room was—at last—the way we wanted it.

"We can't keep this to ourselves," Charles said. "How about throwing a dinner party?"

My thoughts wandered back some 30 years to when my children were young and I had much more going on in my life. And yet we had people in and out of our home virtually every week for picnics, parties, and potlucks. And we loved it.

I missed our open-door spirit. Charles and I had slipped into a predictable routine in recent years, focusing on just the two of us. Now it was clear we both wanted to reinstate the lost art of hospitality. So we did. We started by offering our home for our family's Thanksgiving dinner. And then we volunteered our house for the Christmas party for Charles' coworkers. We also invited our neighbors of four years over for a midweek supper.

Moving and Grooving

Years passed, we grew older, and then we moved several hundred miles away from the home we'd shared for 25 years. That meant new neighbors, community, church, and shopping places. At first I felt overwhelmed. I just didn't have what it took to start over again— much less to drum up the energy for initiating dinner parties and potlucks.

But Charles prodded me. "It's a great way to make new friends," he said with that twinkle in his eye that always won me over. "I'll help. Leave the table and cleanup to me." He had me. I agreed, and we threw a really nice "welcome to the neighborhood" Christmas buffet the first year in our new home. It was a lot of work—but a lot of fun too. Everyone seemed to have a good time.

Neighbors picked up the trend, and the man across the street established an almost-annual practice of barbecuing beef ribs for our little community and inviting the rest of us to add side dishes and desserts. We met in a cul-de-sac, set up tables and chairs and umbrellas, and then ate and talked and enjoyed one another's company. What fun! And all because a few people decided to share the gift of hospitality with all the people in our senior-living neighborhood.

A Sudden Change

Then came the year when Charles' health went downhill quickly. He was diagnosed with cancer and given only a few months to live. The last thing I wanted to do was host people in our home. I knew visitors mattered to him, especially in those final weeks of his life. So I mustered. I spread the word that our house would be open to friends and family who wanted to see Charles one last time, to love on him, and to say goodbye. People streamed in and out over several days, and it was a truly wonderful experience for both of us.

During that period, I discovered that "homespun hospitality," as I like to call it, can come in many different forms. The point is to be with people, to share what we have, and to open our hearts as well as our homes.

After Charles died, my desire to entertain died with him, until 18 months later when I found myself smack-dab in the middle of the biggest pity party of my life. I felt alone, lonely, and listless. I knew the answer. Set the table and invite some friends over. Without hesitating for even a moment, I went to my computer and emailed invitations for dinner to five other single women in my neighborhood.

I prepared my favorite Christmas lasagna, an apple-walnut salad, toasted English muffins, a lemon puff for dessert, and coffee and tea. Afterward we watched *Little Women*, played a gift-exchange game, and then said good night.

I faced a kitchen sink piled high with dishes, cups, glasses, and silverware, but I didn't mind a bit. I had opened myself to something bigger than self-pity. I shared good food, love, laughter, and conversation. My friends still refer to that night as one of the best of that holiday season.

"Let's do it again," said one.

"Great!" I replied. "What day and time should we come to *your* house?" I'm still waiting for her answer.

In 1 Peter 4:9, Peter reminds us to "offer hospitality to one another without grumbling." When you choose to open your home and your heart, you'll find yourself laughing all the way—and your guests will join you.

. . . .

Wit:

"Whether it's the best of times or the worst of times, it's the only time we've got." ART BUCHWALD

Wisdom:

"Do not forget to do good and to share with others, for with such sacrifices God is pleased" (Hebrews 13:16).

Willpower:

"I'm going to get out my best dishes and tablecloth and throw a dinner party! However large or small, I'll bless others and myself with hospitality."

7

Forgiveness, Love, and Respect

Making a Choice to Let Go

"Toward the end of life a universal forgiveness of everything for being what it is becomes the only way we can see and understand reality and finally live at peace." Father Richard Rohr's words speak to me today in a way I wouldn't have understood earlier in my life. I've read books on forgiveness and on the importance of putting aside past hurts. I've realized that I too have done my share of hurting others, as much as I hate to admit it.

To come to a place where we can forgive everything and everyone for simply being the way it is and the way they and we are is *huge*. It goes against our small and petty point of view. We want justice—and in some cases, revenge. We want people to hear our story and take our side. It usually doesn't feel okay to simply forgive without some form of retribution—personal or universal. And yet we're powerless to bring that about.

Trapped by Hurt

"Hurt people hurt people" is often stated in 12-step programs such as Alcoholics Anonymous. How true that is. A mountain of hurt is often behind every attack, whether personal or universal, whether between individuals or between nations.

When someone punches us physically or emotionally, we want to punch back, to defend ourselves, to make sure the other person gets his or her just dessert. For years I held on to grudges against former teachers, my ex-husband and his new wife, a neighbor who lashed out at me for what she saw as meddling in her affairs (something I saw as genuine care), and on and on.

For many of us, especially as we move into our senior years, our wounds continue to hold us hostage. We're still bleeding, weak, in pain, and misunderstood. *Doesn't anyone know how I feel?* is a natural response. *Where's God? Doesn't he care?*

What Now?

It's so easy to look outside ourselves for someone or some situation to pin the responsibility on. Just think of all the conversations you've had over the past few days or weeks. Aren't they generally about people blaming others, finding fault, and rehashing events and circumstances to keep us in the clear? Conversations that show others how wise and good and kind we are? So undeserving of the behavior other people subject us to?

I've been as guilty of this as anyone, but not long ago I discovered that when I hold on to my hurts, I can't move forward. I'm stuck in a whirlpool just trying to survive. That's no way to live. Pride takes over, and often we'll just be darned if we're going to forgive someone who is clearly, as we see it, in the wrong—whether across the world or across the breakfast table. If only they would wake up, listen to us, stop fighting, and apologize, everything would be all right.

Only Love Wins

We can't forgive without God's help. That's the rub. Only God can give us the heart, the love, and the willpower to let another person or group off the hook. God *is* love. And love always wins.

So the only way I can be right with God, with others, and with myself is to love and respect my fellow human beings. They are just like me with human flaws, human faults, and human frailties. Yes, even those people some might consider evil.

I can only take care of myself—and that's a pretty big job in and of itself. Each of us must find our own path to make amends when we become aware of our sins and to entrust one another to God for the hard work of revealing them to us. Look at David and Paul and Peter in the Bible. Each one had to discover for himself "that it is not by sword or spear that the LORD saves; for the battle is the LORD's" (1 Samuel 17:47). And this is just as true today for each of us. Every one of our battles is the Lord's. When I keep my eye on *my* life, I'm more able to give the other person the benefit of the doubt and the love and respect he or she deserves simply for being. But are there exceptions? What about those who overpower other nations? And what about rapists, and adulterers, and liars, and murderers? Surely we aren't expected to love and respect such people?

Actually, we are. Jesus tells us to love our *enemies*. "I tell you, love your enemies and pray for those who persecute you" (Matthew 5:44). Beautiful words to read—not so easy to live by.

A Blind Eye

Recently, I watched a rerun of *Howard's End*, a movie based on the novel by E.M. Forster, with Emma Thompson playing Margaret and Anthony Hopkins playing Henry. One scene in particular captured my attention. Henry, the gentleman and property owner of a country home, Howard's End, refuses to allow his wife Margaret's sister Helen, who is pregnant outside of marriage, to spend a night in their home because in Henry's mind, Helen is a "fallen woman."

Margaret reacts with fury and disbelief as she observes Henry being totally blind to his own sexual indiscretion ten years prior when he was unfaithful to his first wife, an event that Margaret herself forgave him for before she accepted his marriage proposal. Margaret beseeches him to look at his own failure and have compassion for her sister, but he stalks off in defiance, holding on to his hypocrisy. By the end of the movie, Henry comes to terms with his humanity and the humanity and frailty of others. (The closing scene shows Margaret, Helen and her child, and Henry all living together at Howard's End.)

I related to Henry. There have been times in my life when I was so busy looking at the speck in the eye of others that I totally missed the beam in my own (see Matthew 7:3).

Looking to Jesus

Richard Rohr points out that "Jesus was fully at home with a tragic sense of life. He lived, died, and rose inside it…(his) ability to find a higher order inside constant disorder is the very heart of his message, and why true Gospel, as rare as it might be, still heals and renews all that it touches," going well beyond forgiveness for this or that offense.

Words to chew on over and over. It starts and ends with God's unmerited love and grace toward us and toward every one of his children whether or not they acknowledge him. Can we offer others any less than we, who are also imperfect, have been freely given? Let's not wait another day to forgive others—and perhaps more importantly—to forgive ourselves for being human, imperfect, and utterly dependent on the love and care of God, who created each one of us in his image.

. . . .

Wit:

"Forgiveness is the needle that knows how to mend." JEWEL

Wisdom:

"Blessed are the peacemakers, for they will be called children of God" (Matthew 5:9).

Willpower:

"Today I choose to forgive others and myself. I'm grateful for the healing power of this action that is setting me free."

8

Invisible Gifts

Making a Choice to Find What Is Hidden

In the previous chapter I talked about forgiveness. In this chapter, I want to look at the gifts that can flow into our lives as a result of the pain we've forgiven. Sometimes it takes years before we see these gifts because they're hiding out until we're ready to receive them.

Maybe, like me, you've caught yourself saying, "Oh, now I get it. Now I see why I had to go through that heartache. I wouldn't be the person I am today without it." And suddenly we find ourselves being grateful for the very thing we once thought would undo us or the very person we had such a hard time forgiving.

We can also refuse to get it. For some people there's a payoff in remaining the victim of someone else's treatment. When my first husband left our family for another woman, I didn't let go of my bitter feelings for a long, long time because I was trying to squelch them before truly acknowledging them. I feared that if I ever admitted how I really felt, I'd never recover. I thought I was doing the right thing by stuffing away the very thing that was making me sick and keeping me stuck.

I had been happy before my husband left—at least I thought so. My days were simple, predictable, and filled with good things. You know, the things most women long for—a successful husband, children I loved, tennis with my friends three mornings a week, church on Sundays, summer vacations, a lovely home, and a reliable car. What more could I have wanted?

The Gift of Pain

Everything changed the day I watched my husband pack a bag and walk out of our house and our lives. I was sure my life would never be the same again. As the days wore on, I didn't like feeling bitter and resentful day in and day out. I hated his new woman. And I was beginning to hate the man I'd loved for more than 24 years—my husband, my friend, and the father of my children. "How can any good come from this?" I asked over and over. How could they be happy when my children and I were suffering? Then one morning as I jogged along the beach near my home, I turned to God in a fit of panic and fear, begging for help, for grace, for comfort. And he delivered. "Never will I leave you; never will I forsake you" (Hebrews 13:5).

Over time I began to see the *hidden gift* that led to a steady life in Christ, and a new path to freedom that would include spiritual growth, peace, reliance on God—and most important—forgiveness for myself and for my husband and his wife.

Months later, I received a phone call from the woman apologizing for all the hurt and damage she had caused my children and me. It felt good to hear the words I'd longed to hear, but by then they didn't matter as much as I thought they would. God had healed my heart.

The God of all grace, who called you to his eternal glory in

Christ, after you have suffered a little while, will himself restore you and make you strong, firm and steadfast.

1 Peter 5:10

Eventually I remarried and enjoyed many years with a man who was my partner until the day he died. I've been set free of the binding ties of jealousy, anger, and resentment. My son and two daughters have grown and healed, and recently they attended a memorial service for their dad's wife, who died this year. I supported them in prayer as they stood by their dad in his loss.

Recently, I received a note from my ex telling me I'd been a wonderful wife to him, and that he'd never deserved me. He wished me well. Since then, we've become friends, which is good for us and for our children and grandchildren.

Yes, I thought I was happy when I lived that shallow, predictable life decades ago, but now I know *true happiness* is walking one step at a time behind the Great Shepherd.

My life now is filled with one gift after another—many visible and some probably still invisible until I'm ready to see them. Now when something happens to throw me off-kilter, I ask, "What's the lesson here? What is the gift?" How about you? What gifts are now out in the open in your life that had once been hidden?

- Has losing a job moved you to a better career?
- Has the death of a loved one helped you find strength you didn't see before?
- Has a friendship gone south taught you something about yourself that has helped you choose more wisely?
- Has recovering from a health crisis given you insights into the importance of valuing your life?

I'm remembering something I read by the great preacher and

writer Oswald Chambers. He said God doesn't make perfectly shaped grapes; rather, he squeezes the sweetness out of us as the grapes we are. I love that image. As he squeezes, our sweet juice spills onto a world in need, and we are healed in the process. A gift no longer hidden! And one that you can truly smile about.

. . . .

Wit:

"Life always offers you a second chance. It's called *tomorrow*."
Author Unknown

Wisdom:

"'For I know the plans I have for you,' declares the Lord, 'plans to prosper you and not to harm you, plans to give you hope and a future'" (Jeremiah 29:11).

Willpower:

"Today I will look for the hidden gifts in my life, even the ones I may have been too preoccupied to notice before. I will jot them down so I won't forget them."

Part Two

Accepting New Challenges

Challenge: A task or situation that tests someone's
abilities.

NEW OXFORD AMERICAN DICTIONARY

. . . .

Coffee and Tea

Molly, my sister, and I fell out,
And what do you think it was all about?
She loved coffee and I loved tea,
And that was the reason we couldn't agree.

NURSERY RHYME

How silly are Molly and her sister? And how like people all over the
world for all time? We make mountains out of molehills, as the cli-
ché goes. We often create our own challenges by making big things
small and small things big. We forget, even more as we grow older it
seems, that we don't have to agree with others and they don't have to
agree with us. Differences needn't lead to division or conflict. They
can simply *be*. The chapters in this section will focus on the challenges we face when we lose a loved one, have to deal with the people with different personalities, and experience setbacks. We'll also
explore the reasons for taking the road to gratitude.

9

Suddenly Single: Submitting to Grief

Accepting Loss with Dignity

"Hey, Karen."

My church friend Bruce approached and gave me a hug after a Saturday night service. He'd visited my home a week or so before my husband, Charles, died in March 2015. I had just reached the three-month mark of widowhood when we talked.

"How about enrolling in my line dancing class?" he asked. "I teach at the senior center, and I'd love to have you join us. I think it would help you in your grief."

A Step Up—and Out

I was intrigued by the invitation but not sure I was ready to jump back into a social life. I'd tried line dancing some years before and really enjoyed it, but was this the time to start having fun again? What would people think of me? Maybe I should wait a year or so.

But Bruce's slogan, "Dance your troubles away," gave me the courage to step out.

A few weeks later I reserved a spot in his class despite my cautious thoughts. I had so much fun the first six-week session that I signed up again and again, and after a year I moved into the intermediate group. Thanks to Bruce, our class began performing at charity events across our county, drawing others to their feet to dance their troubles away.

An Abrupt and Unwanted Challenge

I learned the Electric Slide, the Boot Scootin' Boogie, the Tush Push, and other dances, and I started to let go and have fun. But then memories of former days intruded—days when Charles and I glided across the dance floor at the Hotel del Coronado some 30-plus years before. We were newly married then and filled with joy, and energy, and love for each other. I'd looked out at our future and knew we had a long life ahead of us.

But then came the day when Dr. Wu closed the door behind him as he entered the small sterile room at his oncology office, where Charles and I sat clutching each other's hands. "I wish I had better news," he'd said, glancing at the oncology report on the computer screen. "Charles, you have late-stage cancer that has metastasized to your liver. We don't know what kind it is or where it originated, so I can't offer any treatment. If I could, I would, I assure you."

After a moment I stuttered a question in a small voice. "Should we call hospice?"

"Tomorrow," he said softy. Then Dr. Wu shook our hands and wished us the best.

We thanked him and wobbled out the door and to the car holding tight to God's grace and to each other.

The following day we enrolled Charles in the program that would sustain us for the next four months.

A New Dance

Grief poured through me that day. We were almost out of time—time to dance, stroll the beach, cook for friends and family, and travel to far-off places. I was going to lose my husband, our marriage would end, and never again on this earth would we share a meal, cuddle in bed, camp by a lake, or sing in the choir.

"I don't want you to go," I sobbed one day as we bumped into each other coming and going from the kitchen. "I want to keep you with me forever."

As I write these words I'm feeling again the deep and unrelenting grief that gripped my soul in that moment. I couldn't imagine my life without Charles at my side. I just couldn't get it. We'd been together for 35 years—nearly half a lifetime.

A New Life—Alone

On March 6, 2015, at 1:30 in the afternoon, my sweetheart died peacefully at home after our children and grands and friends visited him during his final days, loving him, singing to him, and reading Scripture. I'll never forget the hour the undertaker ushered his body out the front door of our house—the place Charles had loved so much and had poured so many hours into, making it a beautiful home for our retirement years together.

Well-intentioned men and women reminded me that I will see him again in heaven, but somehow I didn't find that encouraging. I missed Charles there and then in the flesh. I missed watching him trim our roses, polish my shoes, run a load of laundry, surprise me with a bouquet, catch me with a hug and a kiss when I was overfocused on writing, pray with me, and suggest we eat out on a much-too-busy day.

A New Beginning

I needed help and I knew it. I had grieved for my father years before and then for my mother five years after that, but this shade of grief was different. It was dark, and menacing, and unrelenting. I couldn't get a grip on it. It hit me in the middle of the night, slapped me during a movie, smacked me while having coffee with a friend, and flooded me with tears in front of the clerk at the Social Security office.

I took advantage of the grief support that hospice offered, and I enrolled in GriefShare (griefshare.org) at church. I found it enormously helpful to put words to my sorrow. The more I talked, the better I felt. Some participants couldn't get past their tears. Words clogged their throats. Others left early or stopped coming. Still others said they just couldn't take all the sadness in the room.

"I don't need it," said one of my friends. "I had two years to grieve while Hank was so ill. Frankly, I'm worn out. I want to get on with my life, not sit and cry with strangers."

Another said she and her husband had had a difficult marriage and in some ways she was relieved to be on the other side of it. One of the men voiced his regret over being emotionally closed to his wife while she was alive.

I understood—completely. But I didn't want to quit. I desperately needed to get to the other side of this mountain.

Everyone has his or her own way of grieving, and there is no *one* way that is best. I knew that. I could see it in the room. For some, grief seems to be on hold for months, and then suddenly it breaks through. For others, and I'm one of them, it's essential to talk and cry right from the start, to let out our feelings as we feel them.

A neighbor of mine lost his wife to brain cancer, but he couldn't let the tears come. Instead, he shared funny stories and jokes with whomever would listen. He pushed away the sadness to the point that he jumped into another relationship within a few months after his wife's passing and was engaged to be married before the year was out. But then without warning he woke up one day and was engulfed in grief for his wife. He broke the engagement and moved back to the house he had shared with her—long enough to come to terms with his loss.

A New Wave of Grief

Suddenly, just before I reached the second anniversary of Charles' death, news came that our beloved line-dance teacher, Bruce, was extremely ill. He closed his classes to devote time to recovering his health. But it was not to be. Cancer had invaded his body, and he died just a few weeks later. I couldn't bear it. He had been such a strong man and so full of good cheer. He's the one who had helped me dance my troubles away. And now here I was mourning again.

But God promises to turn our mourning into joy and dancing, so our tribute to Bruce continues as his teaching partner and one of his best students have taken over the class.

Today I am into my third year without Charles, and my first year without my dear friend Bruce, and only a few weeks into the loss of my younger sister, June, who died after a long and debilitating illness. I miss them terribly. I cling to the grace God renews each morning. I'm thankful I have family close by to encourage and support me.

It took time to surrender to these losses and to accept them. As we age, we will lose more of our loved ones. Grief will visit us again and again, and one day we will be the reason for someone else's grief. The challenge, then, becomes not so much one of overcoming sadness, though that's part of it, but of accepting the loss and embracing the promise of God to never leave us nor forsake us regardless of what happens.

I needed help to get where I am today, so I reached for it and accepted it. I did not laugh my way through this agonizing challenge, but I did learn to smile again.

If you are in a similar situation I hope you will seek the support you deserve.

> *Do not fear, for I am with you; do not be dismayed, for I am your God. I will strengthen you and help you; I will uphold you with my righteous right hand.*
>
> Isaiah 41:10

. . . .

Wit:

"If you're on thin ice, you might as well be dancing." Author Unknown

Wisdom:

"A time to weep and a time to laugh, a time to mourn and a time to dance" (Ecclesiastes 3:4).

Willpower:

"Today I will focus on the gift of life—here on earth and here-after—and give thanks for my deceased loved ones who showed me with courage how to live, how to die, and even how to dance."

10

Personality Puzzle

Accepting Temperament Differences

I walked into the convention center in Albuquerque, New Mexico, for a major conference. The attendees, more than 1,800 in total, took up the three major ballrooms. I'd never been to such a large gathering in my life. It was a great opportunity to people watch, something I love to do.

By the time we broke for lunch, I had met and talked with a huge number of men and women and learned so much about their lives, backgrounds, goals, and dreams. It was an awesome experience.

I was also aware of the many differences from one to another. The room was filled to capacity with people from 42 countries and every state in the Union. There were personalities ranging from the playful types who loved to interject a bit of humor into our round-table discussion to the take-charge man who kept trying to return our group to the topic assigned.

And, of course, there were the peaceful people, who smiled and went along with the majority, as well as the ones who liked flexing their power muscles, though no one assigned them the task.

You Know the Types

Think about the personalities in your life—and your own personality, for that matter. The president of your homeowners association, who would rather lead than follow and do things his way instead of risking the mistakes of someone else's. Your spouse, who likes to plan projects and activities so they're completed correctly—the first time. You—you're the casual type, making decisions at the last minute depending on how you feel.

And then there are adult children and friends who dodge unpleasant conversations because they prefer to avoid conflict.

Have you ever looked at life with a big sigh, wishing you had a better understanding of why people, yourself included, behave the way they do? Relationships may seem like a giant puzzle with so many pieces to fit together that you don't even know where to start. Maybe it would help to take a gander at the big picture first. See what it *could* look like. I found that as I began to understand myself, it was easier to understand others and what makes them tick. Here's what I learned that changed for the better all of my relationships, especially as I've grown older.

It's (Not) All Greek

The study of personalities started with the experiences of Greek physician Hippocrates, one of the outstanding figures in the history of medicine, who lived during the Age of Pericles (494–429 BC). He divided the types he noticed into four groups based on his medical observations and findings. The *Sanguine* and *Choleric* personality types tend to be sociable, comfortable in a crowd, and even preferring to stand out. The *Melancholy* and *Phlegmatic* types are reserved, even shy, and often feel anxious about being around too many people at once. They especially don't like to be singled out.

No one is just one type. We all have a little of each. If you want to learn more about the history and science of the personalities, you can find a wealth of information online.

Updating Hippocrates' Findings

Over the years many individuals, including Christian author and speaker Florence Littauer in her Personality Plus training and in her books, have given the four types a modern look. We'll keep with our puzzle theme.

The Playful personality stands out as the bright flower in the puzzle. *Playfuls* (Sanguines) love to get things going—whether at a party or a picnic. They don't wait around for people to make friends with them. They walk right up to men, women, and children and start a conversation. They always have great ideas, and they're full of encouraging words, wanting everyone to have a good time whether at home or at work. The Playful is also up for plenty of fun and adventure. If you need a smile or a hand to hold, look for a Playful. And you can count on him or her to suggest something zany to do on a stormy day when you're stuck indoors.

The Powerful personality types are what you might call the square corners of the puzzle. They generally don't discuss options with others. Why? Because they prefer to lead than follow, motivating people to take action, controlling plans and productivity, and calling out quick and clear instructions so everyone within earshot can't miss the immediate gain. Don't be shocked by their sometimes-bossy nature. It's easy to feel overwhelmed by Powerfuls. Rarely do they realize how they come across. They're just doing what comes naturally to them. You might even feel intimidated in their presence—unless you're one yourself.

On the upside, however, *Powerfuls* (Cholerics) provide structure and boundaries for an organization and for a household. Ask them to take charge of a family vacation or head up a class reunion or an event in your retirement community, and you won't be disappointed by the results.

The outstanding managers, leaders, and supervisors in your life are probably Powerfuls because they welcome being in charge and wouldn't have it any other way. If you're able to support and acknowledge them and cooperate on projects, display your loyalty, and approve their ideas, the benefits will spill into your life too. If you want to grow and achieve your own personal and professional goals, Powerfuls are the ones to watch and learn from. If at times you feel pushed around—well, you might be. For a Powerful, life often comes across as "my way or the highway."

The Perfect personality types frame the puzzle. They make up the straight edges. When it comes to details, details, and more details, these men and women are the perfect choice. They raise their hands for any tasks related to finances, are alert to the needs of others, and keep their attention on coworkers and family members regarding long-range goals of spending and saving wisely. Perfects have to check themselves because they can be critical in their desire to keep things efficient and economical. They are ideal examples of having a place for everything and putting everything in its place. On the flip side, they are also sincere and sensitive people who appreciate being appreciated. Give *Perfects* (Melancholies) what they need—quiet order and absolute understanding—and they'll give you what you want. They're good listeners and loyal friends and family members. They are great with charts, graphs, and budgets.

We learned in Florence Littauer's Personality Plus Training that Charles was a *Perfect* and I am a *Playful.* We had some work to do to steady our marital boat, so we left the weekend workshop with a big sigh and a commitment to do what we needed to do to better understand and relate to each other. Not easy, but doable. At least we now had the tools, thanks to the training, and could get to work right away.

I began to see *why* Charles did the things he did in the way he did them. And he lightened up a bit as he began to see that having fun and smiling more could add some levity to his life. We made it through the next 20 years giving and receiving grace to each other. By the time Charles passed away, we had been at our best for quite some time.

Peaceful personality types cover the landscape of the puzzle. If you need a support team at work or a listening friend to help you bear a burden, you'll find these traits in this personality type. Such individuals find the middle ground despite chaos and confusion. *Peacefuls* (Phlegmatics) are sometimes undisciplined because of their devotion to peace and quiet. They may have a hard time making decisions, but they present a balanced point of view that brings people together in even the most stressful situations.

The Peaceful personality, however, won't rouse a crowd or remind people of deadlines. In fact, he or she is the one to procrastinate more than any other. But he or she is also the ideal one to support and comfort others when morale is low, standing ready to give out big hugs.

Are You an Extrovert or an Introvert?

All the personalities in the puzzle have a basic temperament that drives and motivates them. *Extroverts* are those men and women who love people and have lots of stories to share. They're sociable. They receive their energy from laughing, and talking, and hanging out with others. This fuel keeps them going during the times when they *have* to be alone because of illness, being away from family, or when they're on a job that requires silence and privacy.

Introverts are just the opposite. They crave time alone and are fueled by hours without anyone to keep them company. When they *must* return to the masses at work, in the neighborhood, or on a crowded ballroom floor, they can survive because they're refueled during their quiet time.

However, no one is really either/or but rather a blend of the two with a sharp tendency toward one or the other. You might assume that Playfuls and Powerfuls are extroverts and the Peacefuls and Perfects are the introverts. That may be true for most, but there can be exceptions. Staying alert to people's moods and behaviors and attitudes can tip you off about whether they need to be with others or with themselves to be at their best.

By picking up the signals and words people share, we can get to know them better and enjoy them more. This information also helps us communicate *our* needs in ways that will help others do the same for us.

As Oswald Chambers wrote in his famous book *My Utmost for His Highest,* "Love is the outpouring of one personality in fellowship with another personality."

It takes desire and time to discover and learn about the personality types and to discern which people in your life are extroverts and which are introverts. And you'll want to find out these things about yourself too. God designed each puzzle piece so we'll fit together and have a part to play in this scene we call life. Once you have a good sense of the various personality types and how they interact with one another, you can experience a richer and more satisfying life at home, in church, at work, and in your community.

At the end of my life I want to go out on a high note with my family and friends. I want to be remembered as someone who loved, accepted, and enjoyed them as they were, as they expressed their personalities. And I want to be known as someone who enjoyed life…laughing all the way.

I always pray with joy... being confident of this, that he who began a good work in you will carry it on to completion until the day of Christ Jesus.

Philippians 1:4,6

We have different gifts, according to the grace given to each of us.

Romans 12:6

. . . .

Wit:

"Some people are like clouds. When they go away, it's a brighter day." Author Unknown

Wisdom:

"Just as a body, though one, has many parts, but all its many parts form one body, so it is with Christ" (1 Corinthians 12:12).

Willpower:

"Today I will focus on others and their special gifts. I will not judge them inferior to me just because they may be different in the way they live and express their personalities."

11

The Artist Within

Accepting and Expressing Our Talents

I stood on the platform facing some 300 women at a church retreat in Southern California. I hoped to encourage them to take risks, explore their potential, and release the artist within just as I had taught aspiring writers for many years to release the writer within themselves.

Women clapped and shouted as I shared stories from my life and the lives of others who had taken risks, my husband's friend Manny among them. He spent the first 30 years of his career as an accountant—work he *never* enjoyed. It was a profession his mother talked him into so he could put "bread on the table" for his family. His heart, however, called him to paint and sculpt.

Manny took a big risk in his late fifties by accepting an early retirement package from the firm where he worked so he could do what he loved. He enrolled in a sculpting class and became so expressive in this art form that his mentor turned over the class to Manny whenever the teacher had to be away. Within two years,

Manny sold his first piece for $10,000, more than he'd ever dreamed possible.

When he died 15 years later, Manny was well known in and around New York for his artwork. He passed away a happy man, fulfilled and peaceful.

The Magic of Creativity

Writer Katherine Scott Jones says in her article "Made in God's Image: Becoming Creative Creatures": "We experience something magical when we create. Creativity taps into a place deep inside us that God hardwired into our souls." (See *The Lookout,* June 11, 2017.) God, our Creator, said, "Let us make mankind in our image" (Genesis 1:26).

If God values creativity, how can we not appreciate it too? That doesn't mean each of us will write a book, sculpt, compose a symphony, or paint, but it does suggest that every one of us has something creative to offer the world. Consider inventors such as Thomas Edison (the lightbulb), Steve Jobs (the iPhone), Martin Keyes (the paper plate), and Philip Diehl (the ceiling fan) to name just a few.

We express our creative selves in the arts, science, technology, education, medicine, and so many other ways. And we take big risks doing so. Some people may admire us, and others may see us as shiftless and irresponsible because acceptance and monetary rewards can be slim to none for decades.

"So What!"

I have to say "So what!" to the negative voice that sometimes drowns out the encouraging voice that is also within. Ever since I was in third grade, I knew I would be a professional writer someday. Nothing has quelled that desire or silenced the call. And here I am, some 40 years after I put my first word on paper, thriving, loving, and being deeply satisfied with my creative writing career.

Have you shushed the artist within you?

- Do you long to paint?
- Do you have a book inside you?
- Are song lyrics bursting to be heard?
- Do you have an idea for a time-saving invention?
- Are you dying to put your hands into clay and fashion something beautiful?

Then you *must* give in. If not now, when? The second half of life is the ideal time to take your creative self seriously. Time is running out. The kids are grown and gone. Your professional life may be almost over. Your spouse may have gone on to heaven before you. *It's now or never.* As popular speaker and author Wayne W. Dyer often said, "Don't die with the music still in you."

Spend some time today reflecting on your talent, your gifts, and your desire. What can you do *right now* to lead you in the direction of releasing the artist within you?

. . . .

Wit:

"Every child is an artist. The problem is how to remain an artist once we grow up." PABLO PICASSO

Wisdom:

"He has filled them with skill to do all kinds of work as engravers,

designers, embroiderers in blue, purple and scarlet yarn and fine linen, and weavers—all of them skilled workers and designers" (Exodus 35:35).

Willpower:

"Today I will consider the creative endeavor I *really* want to explore. Next, I will take the first step in realizing that dream: a class, a book, a seminar, a website—wherever I can learn how to get started or take off from where I'm at."

12

Giving Up or Giving In?

Accepting Setbacks

I heard the familiar *ding* on my phone. A text had come in from my daughter Julie. "Mom, I broke an ankle yesterday indoor rock climbing. I'm having surgery tomorrow."

Oh no! We were thousands of miles away from each other. I offered to fly out that day. She thanked me for my love and concern, but she said her oldest son and a good friend could move in with her for as long as necessary. She and I would keep in touch by phone and text. Thank heaven for smartphones.

The break was a real setback. She had an important speaking engagement in Texas the following weekend and had a pile of work to complete before catching her plane. Now would she even be able to go? Of course she couldn't, so the team brought her in via Skype.

My friend Kate's brother-in-law died two days before she and her husband were scheduled to go on a cruise in Europe. He had been hanging on for years, but now suddenly—that day of all days—he slipped away. A setback and a loss.

Randy was terminated when a new company purchased the firm he'd worked for during the past 15 years. He was already 60 and close to retirement. Where would he find new employment with a good salary at this stage of life? A huge setback.

What do we do in these situations? Give up? Give in? Or accept setbacks and carry on? Some people dig in and start repairing their lives and their plans. Others feel helpless to start over. One woman sits in a rocker each day because she can't face life without her husband. Another widow opens her home to grieving wives, and, together, they begin to heal.

Gaining a New Perspective

The 2017 hurricanes towered over a broken ankle, a job loss, or even the death of an individual who suffered a long time, as difficult as it was for the family to lose him.

One mother died in floodwaters while her toddler clung to her back and was saved. Another mother watched the torrent overtake her van and sweep away her four children before she could get to them. When this mother was interviewed on television, the reporter asked her what she wanted people to know about her children. "They were good kids, happy," she said through her tears.

These experiences are more than tragedies. They are losses of epic proportion. And yet some people come through them and are stronger for them, while others sink low and never come back.

How do people get over losing every possession they had and then losing family members too?

Nothing New Under the Sun

Stories of people enduring setbacks today are not unlike those of ancient times. Men and women throughout history have been powerless without God's direction and care, even if they've never had any understanding or knowledge of God before.

- How did Mary, the mother of Jesus, live through the news that she would become the mother of Jesus before she was married? She trusted God.

- How did Hannah bear the shame of being barren for so many years before she became pregnant? She continued to pray.

- How did Ruth and Naomi handle the loss of their beloved husbands? Ruth chose Naomi's God. Then they sought God's direction and made a new life together, which eventually led Ruth into marriage with Boaz—all part of God's plan for her life.

- How did David, a shepherd boy, handle the prospect of facing the warrior Goliath in battle?

- And what about Job being tested, Stephen being stoned, and Paul being imprisoned?

God does not always spare his servants suffering or even death, but he never leaves nor forsakes them.

> *Those who suffer he delivers in their suffering; he speaks to them in their affliction.*
>
> Job 36:15

Yes, in amazing ways, God sometimes takes us in a new direction or to a new location if a house is lost, opens the door to a new relationship after the death of a loved one, or provides a turn in health that leads to healing or a merciful death that ends suffering. And lessons are learned and insights gained that we might have missed had we not gone through these setbacks.

So what is the answer? The *only* answer that provides assurance, protection, and guidance? Turning to God even if our faith is as small as a mustard seed. The promises we read in Scripture may look good on paper and sound inspiring in a sermon, but the impact rarely hits us until we experience a setback so profound and so debilitating that we are truly powerless and then the truth of God's Word can and will set us free if we cling to it and trust it.

Some remain paralyzed in fear or take matters into their own hands and declare war on opposing forces—whether a person, natural disaster, government, some agency, or even God. But as Hannah Whitall Smith says with conviction in her famous book *The Christian's Secret of a Happy Life*, "It is never a sign of a divine leading when the Christian insists on opening his own way and riding roughshod over all opposing things. If the Lord 'goes before' us, he will open the door for us, and we shall not need to batter down doors for ourselves."

As we rest in God, inspiring things can happen: people helping others, sharing even meager resources with neighbors and friends, and finding within ourselves strength we may never have known was there.

Setbacks, however extreme, are just that. They set us back for a time, but only for a time. As long as we are alive we never need to give up or give in, but rather give ourselves over to God and keep on walking—and smiling—all the way.

• • • • • • • • • •

Wit:

"If you aren't in over your head, how do you know how tall you are?" AUTHOR UNKNOWN

Wisdom:

"He gives strength to the weary and increases the power of the weak" (Isaiah 40:29).

Willpower:

"Today I will not give in to the setbacks in my life or give up on God. I will trust the Lord for guidance, and then I will roll up my sleeves and carry on."

13

No One Can Steal Your Joy

Accepting a Joyful Outlook

I remember my grandpa talking to kids and dogs and strangers on the street, in grocery stores, and on the bus.

"Why are you talking to people you don't know?" I asked, feeling embarrassed.

"Because…" he said.

"Because why?" I persisted.

"Because they're people just like us, don't you know," he said. "And we make each other happy when we're friendly," he added in his delightful Irish brogue.

That gave me something to think about. Now as a grandparent myself, I know he was right. Whenever I start a conversation with someone old or young, even exchanging just a few sentences, people respond well. My grandfather set the example with his positive outlook and joyful smile. He didn't let anything keep him down for long.

A Cup Running Over

I recently visited my great-grandson and his mom. The minute I arrived, little Massey pulled me by one finger into the family room. He promptly grabbed his favorite book on trucks, opened the cuddle blanket on the sofa, and motioned for me to sit next to him. He was ready for a good read!

I'd had a tough morning trying to work out details with a contractor for some house repairs, but one smile from Massey and I let all that go and just settled into the joy he shared.

I recall another time when I had a choice to let a disappointment steal my joy or to hold on to it. At the last minute, my adult son canceled his agreement to attend a holiday dinner. My first reaction was hurt and then anger because this wasn't the first time he'd begged off. But I took a breath and found the words I really wanted to say, "We'll miss you, and I love you." The minute I hung up the phone, relief swept over me. Instead of taking the easy road straight into a pity party or playing the shame and blame game, I'd decided to celebrate with those who had shown up. I wouldn't let my son steal my joy. I focused on the lovely meal, the beautiful apartment I lived in at the time, and the holiday in front of me. On the next special occasion my son was at the table sitting right next to me.

No one can steal our joy unless we allow it. As Scripture reminds us, "A joyful heart is good medicine, but a broken spirit dries up the bones" (Proverbs 17:22 NASB).

The next time someone tries to dump a load of guilt on you, or criticizes a decision you made, or finds fault with something you do or say, smile and let it go. Hang on to your joy. It's yours. It's a gift from God, and don't let anyone take it from you. Laugh it off and go on your merry way!

. . . .

Wit:

"To get the full value of joy you must have someone to divide it with." MARK TWAIN

Wisdom:

"You will go out in joy and be led forth in peace" (Isaiah 55:12).

Willpower:

"Today I will be joyful regardless of the circumstances."

14

You Have the Right to Be Wrong

Accepting Vulnerability

I backed out of my parking place in front of the local supermarket and pulled up to the stop sign, aware that the main exit lane had the right of way and also conscious of the incoming cars from Main Street. I looked to my left. All clear.

Beeeeeep! The blast jarred me. I glanced to my right. *Oh no!* I had neglected to recheck the lane to my right and had pulled out in front of a blue car heading for the exit. My fault, absolutely. I felt terrible. I leaned over, held up my hand, and hoped the driver could see my red face. I kept going and he did too, but that sinking feeling I get whenever I'm in the wrong got the best of me. I prayed on the spot that God would help the young man forgive me and that he'd receive a special blessing right then.

This was another strike in a week filled with them. I'd visited a sick friend a few days earlier. As we reminisced about the old days and looked at photos from the past, I commented on how pretty she was in a particular shot. The word *was* offended her.

"What a horrible thing to say!" she shouted. "I could look that way again with a little makeup."

I was astonished. What I intended as a compliment she took as a comparison between past and present. I felt in the wrong. I could have chosen my words more carefully. Maybe I'd spoken too soon. Perhaps I should have nodded and made affirming sounds while looking through the entire album instead of commenting specifically on her appearance.

In the same week I was driving to the beach with a friend, and it appeared she was going to make a U-turn where it was clearly forbidden. I made a remark. She looked at me with a puzzled expression. She was making a left turn, not a U-turn. Once again, my haste, my choice of words, and my lack of diplomacy proved me wrong.

Oh, how I hate to be wrong—even more than I like to be right— which I admit has not been the case lately.

> The three hardest tasks in the world are neither physical feats nor intellectual achievements, but moral acts: to return love for hate, to include the excluded, and to say, "I was wrong."
>
> SYDNEY J. HARRIS

And then there are those pesky unrealistic expectations I indulge in that only lead to disappointment. Like the day a friend asked for a recommendation for a local restaurant. I gave one, only to find out later that she felt ill the following day and was quick to tell me it must have been food poisoning from the dinner house I'd suggested.

I felt wrong again. Maybe her sick feeling had nothing to do with the food or with me, but still I wondered and stewed about it all day.

Okay to Be Wrong?

The older I get, the more I realize how much I don't know. Being willing to revamp my thinking, let go of my prejudices (whatever they may be), and admit I can be wrong more often than not is actually a good thing. Maybe being wrong has a positive side. I'm thinking now that we have the right to be wrong because we are *human beings*, and human beings make mistakes. If we're willing, we can learn from them.

Blind spots, unrealistic expectations, snap judgments, good intentions, and the like can bury us if we let them. But if we acknowledge these experiences and thoughts and opinions as part of a full life, maybe we can go a little easier on people and on ourselves when wrongs occur. Instead of condemning, let's remember that we not only have a right to be wrong, we have a duty to *own* our weaknesses and vulnerabilities. And we have a responsibility to make better choices in the future.

As for me, I will drive more thoughtfully from now on. I'll keep my comments to myself when I'm not sure how they'll be taken. I'll not give driving advice when someone else is behind the wheel. At least those are my plans. But if—when—I blow it again, I'll remind myself that I have the right to be wrong, and then start over again, knowing God's infinite grace and mercy cover me.

. . . .

Wit:

"I'm not arguing; I'm just telling you why you're wrong." AUTHOR UNKNOWN

Wisdom:

"Whatever you do, whether in word or deed, do it all in the name of the Lord Jesus, giving thanks to God the Father through him" (Colossians 3:17).

Willpower:

"Today I will readily admit when I'm wrong and know it. I'll ask God for wisdom and discernment and apologize on the spot."

15

Blessings in Disguise

Accepting Good from the Unexpected

I have a small, framed photo of a little otter on my desk, its front paws perched on a rock in the Monterey Bay, its home and neighborhood. Every time I look at it, I laugh out loud. This little guy and his family and friends are the highlight of my visits to the Monterey Bay Aquarium. They are full of antics, playing with their food, swimming on their backs, grooming the younger ones, and all around appearing to have a good life doing what comes naturally.

So it was with great delight that I read in the fall 2017 issue of *Shore Lines*, the aquarium's member magazine, that Selka, once a shark-bite survivor and research sea otter, had become a surrogate mother to an eight-week-old male pup, as yet unnamed. At first, the caretakers put the two together for a few hours, but Selka didn't seem interested.

The following day she towed the babe around a few times, but then she pushed him aside and refused to share her food. By the third day, Selka began showing the pup a bit of attention, carrying and sharing food with the little newcomer. What a blessing for Selka and the orphaned pup. You might say it was a blessing in disguise for both otters. The mom has a new baby to care for, and the baby has a new mom to love and learn from.

Paying Attention

This story made me take another look at all the blessings that have come into my life disguised in forms I never would have noticed if I hadn't been paying attention. Like the day I became a surrogate grandmother to two children of a close friend, whose father had died suddenly and whose grandparents were gone as well. At first I wondered what I had done, taking on two more grands when I already had eight of my own. But in the decades since, they have been nothing but blessings. It's been my joy to love them into adulthood.

Could the death of my granddog Tanner have been a blessing when I would have much preferred that he get well and stay alive for another few years? Yes. Tanner taught me by example what a gift it is simply to *be.* To accept life and death as it comes. To surrender to my Master as he did to his, asking for little more than food, rest, play, and affection. Who wouldn't give those gifts to a beautiful dog who was part of my family for a dozen years? He had the softest, most velvety ears you'd ever want to pet, and paws that he carefully placed on my lap, reminding me when he needed a good cuddle.

Could the cancellation of a book I had slaved over for months be a blessing in disguise? It meant no publication, no sales, no publicity, no readers, and ultimately no royalty payments. It seemed as though all my work was in vain. But was it? Now I know it was not. I took that book apart, chapter-by-chapter, sometimes story-by-story, and used every bit of the meat for future books and magazine articles. My insights and words did not go to waste. They popped up in fresh ways, and the results were truly blessings in disguise.

What seem to us trials are often blessings in disguise.

OSCAR WILDE, *THE IMPORTANCE OF BEING EARNEST*

Sometimes what we label a "bitter trial" is simply a human error—like the time I baked my first cake for my new husband decades ago, only to discover it burned because I misread the recipe and added only half the liquid called for. It was a new wife's tragedy that day. Later we laughed all the way to the bakery, where I purchased a perfect cake, and we enjoyed a slice with whipped cream and a cup of tea.

It's never too late to laugh at past mistakes and learn from them. It's never too late to discover hidden blessings in what at first seemed like disasters or deep disappointments. And it's always the right time to give thanks in all things to the God who makes all blessings possible for our enrichment, enlightenment, and even entertainment.

. . . .

Wit:

"Looking backwards will cause you to miss out on new blessings ahead." GERMANY KENT

Wisdom:

"No discipline seems pleasant at the time, but painful. Later on, however, it produces a harvest of righteousness and peace for those who have been trained by it" (Hebrews 12:11).

Willpower:

"Today I'm going to pay attention and, instead of getting swallowed in sorrow when something goes wrong, I'm going to look for the blessings in disguise. I will make sure to give God thanks."

16

The Road to Gratitude

Accepting God's Grace

My husband's father, Charlie, loved to share the story of how God provided for his family on Christmas Eve following the death of his own dad when Charlie was 12. His mother had nearly run out of tea and bread that season, and there was no more coal for the stove. The tin box under her bed had only a few coins left, and the straggly Christmas tree in the living room, a gift from the local grocer, held only bits of colored paper that Charlie and his siblings had cut out and hung with care.

But then surprise! That cold night a lone wagon driver dumped a fresh load of fuel into the coal bin and refused to share the name of the donor, as he had sworn to keep the man's name a secret. The family of six had a warm and cozy Christmas after all. They thanked God for his blessings.

That story from the past brought to mind each holiday season in our family the importance of giving thanks always, regardless of the circumstances. And yet in our land of abundance we often forget or we just ignore this daily prayer that could enlarge and enliven our lives if we were more conscious of our blessings.

Box, Bag, or Basket

One way to maintain focus on gratitude is to jot down a few daily blessings and pop them in a little container. Then from time to time read them or share them with your spouse or a friend so you can relive the way God took you through a tough time or surprised you with provisions when you were nearly out of resources. Choose a box, bag, or basket. Pick up a little pad of paper, find a fun pen, and start your gratitude cache.

Remember, sometimes blessings come in ways we don't always recognize unless we stop and pay attention: a beautiful sunset, a bird singing in a tree outside a kitchen window, a child's hug, a cup of tea and a delicious treat. When we wake up to the many, many gifts each day brings, we realize we could spend the entire 24 hours praising and thanking God.

Theologian Henri Nouwen wrote in *The Return of the Prodigal Son* that gratitude is more than a mere thank-you. It's a discipline to be practiced each day in a conscious way. The apostle Paul reminds us in his letter to the Thessalonians, "Rejoice always, pray continually, give thanks in all circumstances; for this is God's will for you in Christ Jesus" (1 Thessalonians 5:16-18).

A Bumpy Road

The road to gratitude, however, is not always the preferred path. In fact, often it is the "road less traveled," but we get so preoccupied with our complaints, wants, wishes, and basic needs that we forget to take the detour that might lead us to the land of serenity and simplicity. When we focus on gratitude, our entire attitude shifts from self-protection and accumulation to peace and contentment.

Here are a few thoughts to inspire you as you choose to walk in gratitude daily.

G.....GRACE

"The Lord God is a Sun and Shield; the Lord bestows [present] grace and favor and [future] glory (honor, splendor and heavenly bliss)! No good thing will He withhold from those who walk uprightly" (Psalm 84:11 AMPC).

R.....RICHES

"The same Lord is Lord over all [of us] and He generously bestows His riches upon all who call upon Him [in faith]" (Romans 10:12 AMPC).

A.....ASSURANCE

"Faith is the assurance [the confirmation, the title deed] of the things [we] hope for, being the proof of things [we] do not see and the conviction of their reality [faith perceiving as real fact what is not revealed to the senses]" (Hebrews 11:1 AMPC).

T......TREASURES

"In Him all the treasures of [divine] wisdom [comprehensive insight into the ways and purposes of God] and [all the riches of spiritual] knowledge and enlightenment are stored up and lie hidden" (Colossians 2:3 AMPC).

I . . . . . . INSTRUCTION

"I [the Lord] will instruct you and teach you in the way you should go; I will counsel you with My eye upon you" (Psalm 32:8 AMPC).

T . . . . . . TRUTH

"[Then] He will cover you with His pinions, and under His wings shall you trust and find refuge; His truth and His faithfulness are a shield and a buckler" (Psalm 91:4 AMPC).

U . . . . . UNDERSTANDING

"Making your ear attentive to skillful and godly Wisdom and inclining and directing your heart and mind to understanding [applying all your powers to the quest for it]" (Proverbs 2:2 AMPC).

D . . . . . DELIGHT

"But his delight and desire are in the law of the Lord, and on His law (the precepts, the instructions, the teachings of God) he habitually meditates (ponders and studies) by day and by night" (Psalm 1:2 AMPC).

E . . . . . ENDURANCE

"May the God Who gives the power of patient endurance (steadfastness) and Who supplies encouragement, grant you to live in such mutual harmony and such full sympathy with one another, in accord with Christ Jesus" (Romans 15:5 AMPC).

With a heart and mind filled with such wisdom, surely we can rejoice all the day through regardless of the circumstances.

. . . .

Wit:

"Feeling gratitude and not expressing it is like wrapping a present and not giving it." WILLIAM ARTHUR WARD

Wisdom:

"Let everything that has breath praise the LORD. Praise the LORD" (Psalm 150:6).

Willpower:

"Today I give thanks for every breath I take and every experience I have. I will say thank you to people as often as possible."

Part Three

Taking New Chances

Chance: A possibility of something happening;
the occurrence and development of events in the
absence of any obvious design.

NEW OXFORD AMERICAN DICTIONARY

. . . .

Tears and Fears

Tommy's tears and Mary's fears
will make them old before their years.

NURSERY RHYME

This nursery rhyme sobered me. I see in myself and in the people around me, especially seniors, how tears and fears can shorten our years. How unfortunate it is to spend our precious time cowering and crying about situations we can't control or cure when life still offers promises and plenty if we simply step out and take a chance. The chapters in this section will invite you to explore, do something new—whether scary or intimidating—and discover how capable you really are when it comes to making new friendships, traveling, relating to adult children and grandchildren whose lifestyles you may not understand or like, keeping your own counsel (instead of advising others), and appreciating silence and its many benefits.

17

Walls, Fences, or Welcome Mats?

Taking a Chance with People

The day Grandpa Ennis came to live with my family was one of the happiest days of my young life. My grandmothers and Grandpa O'Connor had all gone home to God long before I was born, so the only grandparent I knew was my mother's father. He had the softest chuckle, the sweetest smile, and the kindest words of anyone I knew. I also loved to listen to his Irish brogue.

And the sparkle in his blue eyes let me know I was welcome whenever I stopped by his bedroom to chat or to see what he was reading. What I most remember about him was his ability to find humor in any situation. He truly laughed all the way through life, and people who knew him couldn't help but join in.

Grandpa enjoyed telling stories from his childhood in Ireland as much as I enjoyed listening to them. I dreamed of visiting Dublin, the city of his birth, one day. And finally I did in 2012, long after Grandpa had gone to heaven.

A New Kind of Family

Grandpa's move to our house was my introduction to living in the mix—a mix of traditional Mom, Dad, and kids family life to one that included someone from a former generation. Back in the day, grandparents moved in with their kids and grandkids when they grew old. Today, many seniors move to a retirement community or a nursing home far from family when the time comes.

Because of Grandpa I met a lot of older people—his bowling buddy, the man he attended the horse races with, and his friends from church. Before long I thought of them as my friends too.

Doing What Came Naturally

As an adult my perspective on family has expanded well beyond the borders I once knew. I've been divorced, remarried, and now I'm a widow—stations of life I never planned or expected and some not wanted. My extended family-in-love includes a gay stepdaughter and her partner, my son and his wife from Japan, a divorced daughter and her male friend, a sister who was once a nun now married to a former priest, and a sister married to an Italian native and living in Italy, "adopted" grandchildren whose biological grandparents have died, and at one time a Kurdish refugee family with children who referred to my husband and me as their American grandparents.

It wasn't easy to expand my borders. I didn't believe in divorce, and yet there I was, divorced from my first husband. I didn't want to share my neat little life with my second husband's children, and yet there I was, doing just that. I didn't like the idea of my youngest sister settling in Italy so far from our family, and yet there she is—across the ocean from us for more than 30 years.

People make choices. Stuff happens. We either go with the flow, trusting God to take care of what we can't control or we resist and lose relationships that just might help us grow. Regardless, life goes on.

Ouch! Sometimes It Hurts

I've learned, often the hard way, to open my mind and my heart, to put out the welcome mat, and to set the table and prepare a spare bed for all kinds of people. I've also grown in my faith and in my ability to love and include others from various cultures. Each person stretches me in ways that build on the changes and experiences from my life early on. I thank God for nudging me, leading me, and encouraging me to love his people just as he does.

I was surprised to discover I had some hidden prejudices and preconceived judgments I had to put aside. In addition to our blood relations, my husband and children and I welcomed young men and women from other countries, including Germany, Switzerland, and Spain, who lived with us for a time as foreign-exchange students.

My life is now rich in diversity, love, and opportunities because of the experiences I've enjoyed with so many of God's people.

Help and Hope for Living "in the Mix"

For some folks, it's easier to erect a fence, draw a line in the sand, or simply say no to the new and maybe different people who come into their lives, be it by way of marriage, adoption, divorce, or following death. They don't want to disrupt their comfortable lives. Understandable. Especially as we settle into our routines and cling to our ways of thinking about how things should be and how people should behave. But when we put up a fence or place a border around our hearts, we seal off God's love from ourselves and from others.

You may be in a mix too—or maybe you call it a fix. Maybe you provide or participate in an experience of family for some people who are on the fringe of your life, or who are different from you, or whose lifestyle you don't approve of. If so, take heart. God is at the center of it with you. He created and loves you. And he created and loves each one of those "troublesome" people, regardless of their situation or behavior. You can leave the details to him and rest in the knowledge that he will provide everything you need to carry on when the going gets tough.

Here are some Scriptures to cling to and to share with your loved ones as you navigate the waters of living in an unconventional family situation.

- *God's faithfulness:* "I will not violate my covenant or alter what my lips have uttered" (Psalm 89:34).

- *God's help in trouble:* "My flesh and my heart may fail, but God is the strength of my heart and my portion forever" (Psalm 73:26).

- *God's grace in growth:* "Make every effort to add to your faith goodness; and to goodness, knowledge" (2 Peter 1:5).

- *God's correction when necessary:* "Anyone who does not provide for their relatives, and especially for their own household, has denied the faith and is worse than an unbeliever" (1 Timothy 5:8).

- *God's love that covers all:* "God is love. Whoever lives in love lives in God, and God in him" (1 John 4:16).

Borders, fences, or a welcome mat? It's our choice. It's up to each of us. God won't push his agenda. But what a wonderful experience it is to open our heart to the heart of another and say, "Come right in! Welcome to our family."

. . . .

Wit:

"Be yourself; everyone else is already taken." Oscar Wilde

Wisdom:

"He grants peace to your borders and satisfies you with the finest of wheat" (Psalm 147:14).

Willpower:

"Today I will live in harmony with others—especially those who are different from me. We are all God's children."

18

It's Never Too Late for a Playdate

Taking a Chance on Having Fun

"Karen, please teach me how to have fun," my sister June begged with a guilty smile. "I'm too serious, too focused on my work."

I agreed. She was. "Okay, let's start with a weekend camping trip. We can share my tent, walk in the woods, cook over an open fire, and roast marshmallows with the other campers. I have a trip scheduled at Lake Arrowhead over the Fourth of July."

"All right," June replied with a gulp. "I'm in. Sort of…"

We both laughed, hugged, and put the event on our calendars.

One Woman's Play Is Another Woman's Work

June and I arrived at camp, set up my tent, laid out our gear, and trudged up a hill to see what was on the other side. I pulled out my camera and snapped pictures till the sun set. June plopped on the ground and took in a few ragged breaths. This was clearly not her idea of having fun. But then, as she admitted, she didn't have any ideas what fun was. That's why she'd appealed to me for help.

As a university professor, author, and lecturer, June rarely closed the classroom door behind her. I had to tug her sleeve a few times before she got with the program. But she did, and for two days we had a good time trail walking, picking wild flowers, and lounging in our chairs while sipping iced tea.

On the third day, we packed our belongings and headed down the mountain road, happy, satisfied, and ready to relive the experience again. Well, I was, but June not so much. Once was fun. Twice would be work. And she begged off repeating the experience by referring to her advanced age of 60! (Remember, June is my *younger* sister.)

"Play is perceived as unproductive, petty, or even a guilty pleasure," according to Margarita Tartakovsky, MS, associate editor of *World of Psychology.* "Our society tends to dismiss play for adults," she says. The notion is that once we reach adulthood, it's time to get serious. And between personal and professional responsibilities, there's no time to play.

"But play is just as pivotal for adults as it is for kids. Play brings joy. And it's vital for problem-solving, creativity, and relationships." These are fine words from the world of psychology, but I was curious about what the Bible says on the topics of joy and play.

James tells us, "Every good and perfect gift is from above, coming down from the Father of the heavenly lights, who does not change like shifting shadows" (James 1:17). It seems clear that fun, play, and rest are among God's "every good and perfect gift from above."

Play as You Wish

There are so many ways to play. Sewing, card games, sports, collecting stamps, or dolls may be one person's idea of relaxation but the last thing someone else would even consider. My friend Lisa spends her evenings knitting. She has fun choosing patterns and then giving away some of her creative pieces.

Doug and Sherry play Ping-Pong.

My son enjoys a game of pool.

Jane and Dave walk their dogs at the beach and play Frisbee on the sand.

If you're up for fun, you can find it countless ways with a variety of people who share your interests. Square dancing, woodworking, beach volleyball, and collecting shells are just a few of the ways you can enjoy a playdate.

If you're the more sedentary type, find enjoyable activities to do close to home. Visit art galleries and museums, grow flowers and vegetables, join a music appreciation club in your community.

Let's give thanks to God for dancing, and singing, and camping, and hiking, and reading good books, and attending great concerts, and traveling to new places. And, of course, laughing all the way!

. . . .

Wit:

"When nothing is going right, go left." AUTHOR UNKNOWN

Wisdom:

"Let them praise his name with dancing and make music to him with timbrel and harp" (Psalm 149:3).

Willpower:

"I will *play* today—and invite someone to join me!"

19

One Is Silver and the Other Gold

Taking New Chances with Friends

In the early '70s my family moved to a new hillside community. My three children were young, my husband had recently passed the bar exam and was now practicing law, and I was a wife and mom trying to find my place in the world. I was excited about our brand-new four-bedroom house but at the same time bereft leaving my long-time friends and familiar neighborhood. A sweet neighbor came to the door one sunny afternoon and welcomed me with a delightful mixture she dubbed "Friendship Tea." We met over a "cuppa," as the Brits say, and homemade cookies. Life settled down after that. I had a new friend who was making the same adjustments I was.

Another time I met a caring older woman at a women's retreat at the church I attended. She listened to my sad story about a heartache in my life at the time. The two of us had a good cry over a pot of mint tea. By the time we dried our eyes, we were ready to smile. After sharing our struggles, life didn't seem so tragic after all.

Scripture has a lot to say about how friendship can help us

through tough times when we need someone to share our grief or joy with. I've returned to the following verses often over the years.

- "Two are better than one because they have a good return for their labor: If either of them falls down, one can help the other up. But pity anyone who falls and has no one to help them up. Also, if two lie down together, they will keep warm. But how can one keep warm alone? Though one may be overpowered, two can defend themselves. A cord of three strands is not quickly broken" (Ecclesiastes 4:9-12).

- "I have called you friends, for everything that I learned from my Father I have made known to you" (John 15:15).

> There is nothing on this earth more to be prized than true friendship.
>
> THOMAS AQUINAS

> A friend is what the heart needs all the time.
>
> HENRY VAN DYKE

Recently, I heard a discussion on National Public Radio about friendship. A caller stated she had to start drawing boundaries with a few of the women in her life because they were weighing her down with their negative comments and attitudes about life and the aging process. She felt used and abused.

That started a rich conversation between the host and various guests and other callers about the value of friendship, including when it's time to call it quits with some people for whatever reason.

I started thinking about the women and men in my life whom I once considered close friends but have since fallen away (or did I push them away?) for one reason or another—death, relocation, illness, unresolved conflict, an unfulfilled need, or lack of common interests. I feel a pang when I think of some of them now. How could such a change occur when the bond at one time had been so strong?

Relationships are complicated. We don't always wrap up each relationship with a red bow. Some simply go away from neglect, a one-sided passion, a change of heart. I see now that just as we let go of some gifts we once delighted in, we also need to let go of friendships that no longer serve either person.

Long Ago and Far Away

When I was a shy and quiet schoolgirl, I remember feeling lucky when other kids wanted to be my friends, as though I didn't have anything to do with attracting them or creating the relationships between us. I felt honored that they had picked *me*! Poor little Karen. But that's not the case anymore.

Now that I'm an older adult, I'm considering Robert Louis Stevenson's words in a new light: "A friend is a present you give yourself." I realize that yes, *each one of my friends is a gift I give myself*, one to be enjoyed, respected, and appreciated, as well as one to invest in and to be truthful with, as suggested on the NPR radio show. And also one to hold lightly so that if a time comes when we are no longer in sync, we can let go with love and be grateful for what we had.

A Loss Recovered

Sometimes friendships go the other way. Former friends return at a new time and for new reasons. They're to be welcomed too. I had such an experience after my husband Charles died. A caring phone call prompted a renewed connection between one woman and me. And a couple I hadn't seen or heard from in ages was suddenly on my doorstep with a meal, and flowers, and condolences, and a new and deeper regard for me. I felt so blessed.

Just as there are gifts for special occasions, there are friends for special occasions. I have women to walk and talk with, to shop and see movies with, to line dance with, to enjoy a meal with, to pray for and with, and to hang out with from time to time for no particular reason. Not all of them can be all things to me. Nor can I be all things to each of them.

Now that I am widowed, my friends have become more important to me. I relish the variety of interests these women and men have brought into my life, as well as their warmth, advice, playfulness, curiosity, and intelligence. I'm richer for knowing each one.

People come and go in our lives. Some for a season, some for a reason, and some for a lifetime. Friendship is something any of us can have by enlarging our circle of love to include everyone.

I remember singing a fun song with my Girl Scout troop when I was a kid. The lyrics reminded us to keep on making friends—not to limit ourselves to a few. Some friends are as dear as silver, and some are as treasured as gold. And when we realize this truth in our own lives no matter our age, we can turn any frown into a big smile.

. . . .

Wit:

"Friends are chocolate chips in the cookie of life!" AUTHOR UNKNOWN

Wisdom:

"Walk with the wise and become wise" (Proverbs 13:20).

Willpower:

"Today I will get in touch with at least one friend and make plans to spend time together."

20

GRAND Parenting

Taking New Chances as Parents and Grandparents

I've never had a living grandmother. I longed for one, especially when my friends shared about a weekend at their grandparents' house or a trip to Grandma's farm or apartment in the city. Such adventures sounded wonderful and full of fun.

Some of the fantasies of having a grandmother I enjoyed while a kid persisted even into my older years. I longed to whip up a batch of chocolate chip cookies with the grandmother of my dreams. I could fall into her full, soft arms at any time of the day or night, especially when I felt tired or scared.

As I've mentioned, my mother's father lived with our family most of my growing up years, and I loved him dearly, but I never got to go to *his* house. I do remember with affection helping my grandpa pick dandelions out of the backyard lawn and plant a victory garden after World War II.

If you've never had a grandfather to call your own, you might have thoughts about helping him build a tree house in your backyard. There are plenty of opportunities to reach out to help children through your church or community organizations.

Giving and Receiving

What we never experienced with our own grandparents we may hope to give to our grandchildren. Or if we did have idyllic grand-parents, we may want to live by their example. But how realistic is that in today's fast-paced culture when life is on the go 24/7? There may be many grandparents who still fit those pictures, and if so, that's pretty cool. But what about grandmothers, like me, who can't or don't bake anymore? Or grandfathers who will gladly drive a car-pool but should seldom pick up a hammer or position a two-by-four? Can they be *grand*parents in other ways? Yes! There's room for all of us.

Parents of adult children, grandparents of those children's chil-dren, and beyond if we live long enough come in different shapes and sizes and personality types. Each person has something special to bring to the relationship table. What is unique about your place? What do you most like? What do you dislike?

I'm *Me* and You're *You*

At the top of the list of the special things you bring to relation-ships include you. I believe it's essential to be yourself—because all the other "selfs" are taken! Settling into your relationship with your adult children as parents in their own right, and then your grand-children and any new members to the family that come with these roles, takes some doing. But once we relax and realize there are no "musts" or "shoulds," we can become as comfortable with them in our new roles as we would a cozy pair of house slippers.

Stereotypes are out. Individuals are in. That's good news for those of us who are still active in our careers, traveling, volunteering, going back to school, or taking up a new and exciting hobby. One grandmother I know is studying piano for the first time. A grandfather is learning Spanish. Another woman opened a yarn shop, turning her knitting hobby into a profit-making venture. Still others are enjoying freedom from work, giving more time now to family and friends.

The important things haven't changed, namely our presence in the lives of our grandchildren and their parents exactly the way we are and the way they are. You may not bake cakes, but if you can play tag, or climb a rope wall, or read a story, or braid hair, or rustle up a barbecue, you'll find some takers. Let your grandchildren and their parents know what you can and want to do and what you're available for. And, most important of all, that you love them.

Be sure to also express what you're *not* open to. I believe more relationships are spoiled due to unrealistic expectations than for any other reason. It's okay to have a life of your own, a life that includes your grandchildren and their parents as well as other people and activities that matter to you.

More often than not, what children and their moms and dads want most are a listening ear, a warm hug, an "I love you," a pat on the shoulder, and words of encouragement. These are things we all can give.

Don't Forget the *Grown* Kids

To me, grandparenting includes continuing to parent our grown children too. I've met parents who are jealous of the relationship their parents have with the grandkids. They crave some of that special attention. And everyone from both generations wants to be respected for the adults they are, capable of making decisions that are right for them at their age and ability.

Recently, I spoke to two grandparents who were very put out because their adult children weren't taking their advice.

"What good does it do to talk to them?" said the woman.

Her husband joined in with a harrumph. "They don't listen anyway."

"Just as we didn't listen to our parents, right?" I quipped.

The woman stopped and gulped. "You're probably right."

Her husband frowned but then cracked a reluctant smile.

We all enjoyed a good laugh.

We'll never have things just the way we want them, but we can *love* each other to the best of our ability and then rest, trusting God to make all things right in his own way and time.

Perhaps the very best way to become a *grand* parent and *grandparent* is to consider the words of this verse in Deuteronomy: "Only be careful, and watch yourselves closely so that you do not forget the things your eyes have seen or let them fade from your heart as long as you live. Teach them to your children and to their children after them" (Deuteronomy 4:9).

Take a chance. Be your authentic self, and you'll be the *grandest* of parents and grandparents. And if you live as long as some, great-grandparents too. More reason to keep smiling, laughing, and giving thanks!

. . . .

Wit:

"Oh, what a tangled web do parents weave when they think that their children are naive." OGDEN NASH

Wisdom:

"Start children off on the way they should go, and even when they are old they will not turn from it" (Proverbs 22:6).

Willpower:

"I will text, call, write, and visit my adult children and grand-children to check in. I want to be part of their lives while I can."

21

'Trippin' on Trekkin'

Taking New Chances Through Travel

From Belfast, Northern Ireland, to Dublin, Ireland; from Portland, Oregon, to Ketchikan, Alaska; and from Montreal, Quebec, to Boston, Massachusetts, I've been trippin' on trekkin' for the past decade. I have *loved* every minute. Whether on a tour bus visiting United States national parks or on a small ship cruising the Danube River, for me there is nothing like the excitement and the insights new places and new experiences offer to anyone willing to see what's beyond their own neighborhood.

I slurped hearty potato and leek soup in one café, stayed in a funky old hotel in one small village, watched German dancers and singers perform on a ship, panted my way to the top of a medieval castle step-by-crooked-step, and strolled the streets of quaint towns and villages. And I'd do it all over again in a heartbeat.

See What God Has Made

I remember years ago reading about a woman in her golden

years who had raised a family, retired from her career, and was now a widow with time on her hands. She decided to venture out to see what there was to see. She told her children she was going to travel as much as she was able until God called her home. And that's what she did until her final voyage from earth to heaven.

Do you have a spirit of wonder and a bit of wanderlust? Or maybe you want to travel but hesitate for a whole bunch of reasons: you want to save money; lack a travel companion; have anxiety about leaving home; worry about weather, language limitation, food hesitations; and struggle with other things that keep you anchored to your house.

And yet maybe you yearn for the courage and get-up-and-go necessary to make it happen? Why not decide *now* to take a step outside your comfort zone and just do it? Do it whether or not you have a partner? I did that last year, and it turned out to be one of the best experiences of my life. From now on I'm committed to traveling with a group. Single status is right for me at this time. What would you most like to do when it comes to going out and about? Armchair travel at home? A seat on a tour bus or train? Traveling in a camper or with a tent? Whatever your preference, how about just *doing* it?

Hop on the Internet and check out bus tours, walking tours, hiking tours, train tours, and bicycle tours. There is so much to see and enjoy almost anywhere you are or go. And the possibilities for making friends are endless as you explore the great outdoors either in your own country or across the globe. There is something for everyone. And the more you travel, the more you may discover how much there is still to learn no matter how much you know or how old you are. And the more you know, the more reasons for smiling the days away as you realize God's many gifts to us through the culture and history of places well outside our own backyards.

. . . .

Wit:

"The great pleasure in life is doing what people say you cannot do." WALTER BAGEHOT

Wisdom:

"The LORD will watch over your coming and going both now and forevermore" (Psalm 121:8).

Willpower:

"I'm going to choose a place I want to visit—be it ten miles from home or across the globe—and make plans to do it."

22

Yes, You Can Say Yes!

Taking New Chances to Go for It

Do you happen to remember the opening words of M. Scott Peck's bestselling book *The Road Less Traveled*? "Life is difficult." And to that he added at the beginning of the sequel, *Further Along the Road Less Traveled*: "Life is complex."

To his words I add: "Life is complicated." Life is multilayered. It's unpredictable. So why say yes to life? There are just so many challenges and difficulties and unplanned experiences and events that keep us reeling, we might feel it's not worth the effort.

I enjoyed pondering this question for myself as I thought about the people I know and those I've read about, who clearly have said yes by their actions and by their attitude. Mother Teresa comes to mind—as well as Eleanor Roosevelt, Harry Truman, and Dietrich Bonhoeffer, to name a few others. Why did they choose a positive outlook despite health challenges, persecution, aging, family commitments, death of loved ones, disappointments, and personal tragedies?

Despite the circumstances, life becomes easier, more satisfying, and ultimately more joyful when *we choose to embrace it* for what it is and is not instead of resisting it. I remember my mother modeling yes in her life. She always had a smile and a hello for everyone, whether in an elevator or at the park. She took after Grandpa in that way. "We all have problems and pain in our lives," she often said. "If we can lift up one another a bit with a nod or a word of encouragement or a yes, why not? And it makes me happy to do so." Then she'd laugh. "It takes a few years of living to know when to say yes and when to say no. That will come to you too as you grow older and can take care of yourself."

She once told me that whenever she thought about her own mother's life as an Irish immigrant and the hardships her mother had endured, she felt enormously blessed by comparison. "My life today is something my mother could never even have imagined, so I want to say yes to life every chance I get."

It's only in my mature years that I truly understand what she was telling me. A person can live a full, happy, generous life and still be discerning about when to say yes and when to say no.

Living a Yes-Filled Life

How can you say yes to life? What new chances can you seize? How might you change a no or a maybe to a yes? How might you enrich your life as well as the lives of others?

Richard Foster reminds his readers, "If we fill our lives with simple good things and constantly thank God for them, we will know joy." After reading his bestselling book *Celebration of Discipline*, I decided to start filling my life with simple good things, including:

- a smile for everyone I come in contact with each day

- thank-you notes to people who have blessed me with their friendship
- a long daily walk with deep breaths to refresh my body and mind
- reading at least a chapter a day of a book I enjoy (I love cozy mysteries)
- perusing a few pages a day of Scripture and a devotional that inspires me (*My Utmost for His Highest* by Oswald Chambers and any book by Richard Rohr)
- healthy food and plenty of water
- a good night's sleep and a nap when I need it
- line dancing at least once a week with friends
- taking a risk with and for people

I tried an experiment days ago while going for a walk along the beach near my home. I decided to greet every person I met along the way, hoping they'd return my hellos and good mornings but not sure they would. Life is difficult in our country right now, and a lot of men and women are scared, worried, and heavyhearted. To my surprise and delight, each person greeted me in return. I felt my spirit rise a notch and my smile broaden. By the time I walked back to my car, I felt positively buoyant. *Such a simple gesture*, I thought, *and yet such an easy one to make. Why don't I do this every day?* So I decided to do it. Rarely does a person look down or away when I acknowledge him or her. And when that happens, I say to myself, "That's okay. I reached out. I said yes to life in that moment. That's all I can do. At least I'm smiling and laughing."

. . . .

Wit:

"Sometimes you succeed…and other times you learn." ROBERT KIYOSAKI

Wisdom:

"All you need to say is simply 'Yes' or 'No'" (Matthew 5:37).

Willpower:

"Today I will say yes to life and to the gifts and opportunities God brings to me."

23

Hands Off Other People's Everything

Taking a Chance to Set Healthy Boundaries

A woman with lovely blue eyes, graying hair, and expressive hands set up a tent card on a long table at the conference, and then another and another, each one with a printed slogan. One particular slogan caught my attention and has stuck with me all these years: "Hands off other people's everything." *Such a bold and direct statement.* What did that really mean regarding relationships? Was I supposed to let my loved ones sink or swim when I might have words or actions that might help them? *Yep!* That was the point. I soon discovered that keeping our hands off is a sign of respect, trusting God, not ourselves, to lead people in the way they should go.

In our culture there are "boundary crashers" at every turn. Parents steering their grown children against their will, friends telling friends what is best for their lives, clergy giving advice for right living as though they had divine wisdom. We trample lines drawn in the sand; we knock over stop signs; we open doors that say, in effect, "Do Not Enter." And then we wonder why our advice, our terrific ideas, our suggestions are unwelcome. We wonder why those we love and want to be with turn the other way or even walk off—sometimes for good. Let's not take a lifetime to learn the wisdom of "hands off" when we can know freedom for ourselves as well as for others now.

I read recently that the great writer Oswald Chambers discovered a colleague was stealing from him. Instead of confronting the man, Chambers prayed, trusting God to take care of it. One day the man came to Chambers and admitted his theft. Chambers had taken his hands off the situation, letting God do the convicting. After reading about this event, I realized how often I try to accomplish what only God can.

A Painful Lesson

"Hands off" hit home too because I was reminded of the day I learned about relationship boundaries—and not from a painless book or sleep-through lecture. I'd befriended a visitor to a church group I attended. It was obvious she was struggling and needed someone to talk to, a ride here and there since she was without a car, and, perhaps, a family to embrace her until she found a job and a place to live.

I got onboard without a second thought or a prayer. I invited Dodie to our home for a holiday dinner. I took her shopping and paid for some of her small purchases. I drove her to and from medical appointments. I was more than happy to share my blessings, never once considering that I was doing for Dodie some things she was capable of doing herself. As a result, she started depending on me to the point where I began to feel resentful—and then guilty for feeling that way.

Her phone calls poured in, and then bids for attention, and

then crying jags, and then…The general invasion of my life over-whelmed me. I'd wanted to be a friend, not a caretaker. But every time I decided to pull back, I couldn't bear leaving Dodie in the dust. *The least I can do is share my overflow with this poor soul who had so little,* I'd tell myself. When I found out she'd been drinking, I became even more determined to help. I told her about Alcoholics Anonymous. I took her to a prayer meeting for healing. I spent hours talking to her about how she could straighten out her life with God's grace if she would ask him. No change.

Then came the day when I broke down in tears on the phone with my pastor. I shared the situation with him and said I couldn't take one more phone call, give one more ride, or listen to one more sob story. Was there something wrong with me that I was being so selfish?

Learning the Hard Way

That day my pastor taught me a simple lesson I've never forgotten, and it led me to what I now know about creating personal boundaries. "Karen," he said, "if what you are doing for Dodie brings you energy and joy, then you know it's the Holy Spirit leading you. But if it's wearing you down, then it's not from the Spirit. You need to stop and give Dodie to God. He will not desert her."

I thanked him, breathed a sigh of relief, and got together with Dodie to let her know I had no more personal resources to share. I encouraged her to speak to one of our church deacons for help. Instead, she chose to leave the church.

From that point on, I began paying attention to God's voice instead of mine when it came to relating to others. I was beginning to see that I really needed to keep my hands to myself unless directed by the Lord to do otherwise.

SETTING BOUNDARIES CAN HELP US PERSONALLY

Knowing who we are in Christ—our strengths as well as our limitations—helps us to love, care about, and nurture ourselves without falling apart. We won't overstep, overtake, or overdo. We'll give out of our fullness, instead of out of our ego. That means we can say yes or no to requests and opportunities without feeling guilty or overwhelmed. Imagine the freedom!

The Bible says: "Each one should carry their own load" (Galatians 6:5).

SETTING BOUNDARIES HELPS OTHERS

Our family, friends, colleagues, and neighbors will feel and see *our* boundaries, and that may inspire them to look at their own property lines. They may discover more about themselves and who and what they really believe in, care about, and feel. Taking care of one's self *first* is not selfish or unloving when it comes to setting healthy boundaries. The opposite is true. It's being honest and true to oneself, an example of how to care for ourselves as God directs.

One year my young adult son got into debt over an unwise choice. He asked me for a loan—not the first time. He needed $600 right away. By that time I'd learned what it meant to establish a healthy boundary between us, especially around money. I agonized for a short time but then knew what I had to do—for his sake and for mine. I turned him down. He was furious with me and accused me of being an uncaring and unfeeling parent. I nearly caved in at his harsh words, but I knew it would be a mistake to allow him to manipulate me. I'd already bought him a used car, a desk, and a uniform for his new job. That was my limit.

I told him, "I'll always love you and pray for you. But no more loans. I trust you can work out this dilemma on your own." He slammed down the phone. Two weeks later he called, apologized for the way he'd spoken to me, and said my refusal had been the best thing that had happened to him that week. He'd worked out a way to pay off his debt.

The Bible says: "Each of you should give what you have decided in your heart to give" (2 Corinthians 9:7).

SETTING BOUNDARIES INSPIRES INTIMACY WITH GOD

When we're attentive to ourselves, we're in a better position to hear what God is telling us to do or not to do. For example, one evening my husband and I enjoyed a meal with some new friends. Edna talked about a situation in their family that was painful. I found it easy to admire how she'd handled it. "I stayed out of it," she said, smiling. "It's not in my boat."

Her husband, Bill, looked on and agreed. "That's right. We're learning to take care of what's in our own boat, and leaving other people—even if they are related to us—to take care of what's in theirs."

In other words, hands off other boats or as the title of this chapter states, "Hands Off Other People's Everything." Oh, but sometimes it's more fun to row another's boat, or to pick and choose what we think people should keep and what to toss. And sometimes we take their stuff into our boats so they don't have to row or work so hard. Oh, dear! Occasionally, we're our own worst enemy—the pirate at the helm, ready to take over someone else's ship while our own is sinking.

When we row for others or take their burdens and put them in our boat (children who have quit school, run up debt they can't pay off, or hang out with people who are unsavory), we're trying to do for them what only they (and God) can do. We're assuming we know more about how to resolve their problems than God does.

Oh, that statement hurts when I read it. Was I really that much of a meddler? Yes, I was.

But even most important, I'm taking my eyes off rowing my own boat when I'm looking at someone else's.

The Bible says: "Let your conversation be always full of grace, seasoned with salt, so that you may know how to answer everyone" (Colossians 4:6).

SETTING BOUNDARIES IS A GOOD WAY TO WALK WITH JESUS

Jesus taught us by example from his life on earth. I love to review the following verses from time to time, especially when I feel confused about what to do. I look at what he did and then I know when I'm either on the right path or on a path of my own.

- Jesus ate natural foods, got enough sleep, including naps, walked everywhere, and took time to be alone.

- He never hurried. Even when he heard that his good friend Lazarus had died, he didn't rush to the grave. He took his time and arrived ready to perform the miracle of raising the man to life.

- He trusted his Father's will even in the face of the tyranny of the cross.

- He made time for communion with his Father, despite the crowds.

- He responded to baiting questions with insightful questions of his own without becoming defensive.

- He welcomed little children who crowded around him whether or not they cried or squirmed as little ones do.

- He responded to his mother's request to turn water into wine, but he did so when the time was right for him.

He also taught us how to set boundaries by providing clear directions:

- *Ask questions instead of giving advice.* "What do you want me to do for you?" (see Matthew 20:29-34). "Do you want to get well?" (see John 5:1-14). Do you believe? (see Mark 9:17-27).

- *Offer grace and forgiveness.* "Go now and leave your life of sin" (John 8:11).

- *Speak honestly and directly.* "Do nothing out of selfish ambition or vain conceit. Rather, in humility value others above yourselves" (Philippians 2:3).

- *Stay away from deceivers and manipulators.* He cleared out the temple of those who were exploiting the poor (Matthew 21:12-17; John 2:12-16).

Setting healthy boundaries takes time, commitment, study, and practice. For more help, Christian authors Henry Cloud and John Townsend have written a variety of books on the subject, and the series *Setting Boundaries* by Allison Bottke is available.

Whenever I catch myself thinking I have the power to help someone live a better life, I stop and laugh. Who am I to take such an arrogant thought seriously? We can offer bread, but we can't *make* another person eat it. And no one can make me eat the bread someone else offers.

Today I'm living a peaceful life—focused on personal growth, sharing my life with others (without imposing advice unless sought), and in many ways being happier and more joyful than at any other time in my life. I've lifted the burden of my meddling off others and off myself. Instead of giving unwanted advice and rules to live by, I'm resting in the grace of God. And you know what? I'm laughing more—at myself—and that's a good thing.

. . . .

Wit:

"It's better to have your nose in a book than in someone else's business." Adam Stanley

Wisdom:

"We hear that some among you are idle and disruptive. They are not busy; they are busybodies" (2 Thessalonians 3:11).

Willpower:

"At least for today I will keep my hands to myself!"

24

Shhh! The Gift of Silence

Taking the Chance to Speak Less

A wise old owl sat in an oak.
The more he heard the less he spoke.
The less he spoke the more he heard.
Why aren't we all like that wise old bird?

This old English nursery rhyme offers a simple reminder to listen more and speak less, not a popular pastime in our talkative, social media–saturated culture, right? Brother Lawrence, a lay brother who lived in a Carmelite monastery in Paris during the seventeenth century believed that useless thoughts, self-focus, penance, and self-mortification are all unnecessary. Practicing the presence of God in *all* one's affairs and often in silence was the only thing that, for him, made for a quiet life of love, joy, and peace even as he worked in the kitchen as a humble cook. "I possess God (there) in as great tranquility as if I were on my knees."

His was the kind of life Paul talks about in 2 Thessalonians 2:15-16, and one that I want to live.

Take Time to Think Before Speaking

Often, we start talking to fill an awkward moment, or an empty space, or just to hear the sound of our own voice, hoping what we say may help others (or even impress them). But when we take a minute to gather our thoughts before sharing them, we may find what we thought was important simply isn't. This can be especially true when we're tempted to dole out advice to our children or grandchildren. My motto is simple: If they don't ask, don't give.

Take Time to Really Hear the Other Person

When we're tempted to override our friend or spouse or other relative with a story of our own, we need to stop for a second and tune in to what the other person is saying. Will our words add something valuable or will they take away? More often than not, a caring nod or smile is all it takes for the other person to feel heard.

Take Time to Pause During a Conversation

Take a deep breath, smile, make eye contact, and rest. I've been a talkative person most of my life, but in my later years I'm realizing the value of a pause. It gives each person an opportunity to regroup, so to speak, and to decide what comes next. I remember an old boyfriend of mine saying, "You know, Karen, we can enjoy each other's company in the quiet as well as in conversation." Oops! He nailed me on that one.

The gift of silence is a gift like no other. It keeps on giving—in ways we can't imagine until we receive and open it. Take a chance.

Speak less and listen more and see where it takes you. You just might end up like that wise old owl in the tree.

. . . .

Wit:

"Silence is golden. Too bad nobody is buying." AUTHOR UNKNOWN

Wisdom:

"Make it your ambition to lead a quiet life: You should mind your own business and work with your hands" (1 Thessalonians 4:11).

Willpower:

"At least for today I will make a point of speaking less and listening more."

Part Four

Opening New Chapters

Chapter: A period of time or an episode in a person's life.

NEW OXFORD AMERICAN DICTIONARY

. . . .

There's a Neat Little Clock

There's a neat little clock,
In the schoolroom it stands,
And it points to the time
With its two little hands.

And may we, like the clock,
Keep a face clean and bright,
With hands ever ready
To do what is right.

NURSERY RHYME

I love the cadence and message of this sweet Mother Goose rhyme that is obviously aimed at children. Or is it? At every age we're continually challenged to do what is right, and good, and honest. As we live out our golden years, may we keep on opening new chapters that honor God, others, and ourselves with right living. Let's encourage ourselves to focus more on the Lord and less on people and the things of the world, to live simply and honestly, to rest and sleep, to care for our health, and to recognize what a privilege it is to experience our senior years.

25

Becoming Friends with God Again

Opening a New Chapter with the Lord

I grew up in a faith practice that didn't include all the dear old hymns of the church, so when an opportunity came about to participate in a British American Hymn Sing Tour of England and Wales, I knew I had to go. My eyes misted as we landed in Manchester, England, one brisk morning in September 2013. I knew this was going to be a trip of a lifetime visiting the places where some of the great Christian hymn composers had lived, worked, and worshipped.

Among my favorites was Frances Ridley Havergal (1836–1879), author of "Take My Life and Let It Be," and other beloved worship songs. My heart pounded as the tour bus pulled into the town of Stourport along the Severn River to the village of Astley one late afternoon. Frances was born in the rectory of Astley Church, where her father, William Henry Havergal, had been the rector.

Even from her youngest years, Frances was devoted to Jesus Christ. She had little interest in the world. She turned down marriage proposals and a fancy lifestyle. Frances even sold her jewelry, using the money to support her dedication to sharing the gospel through her hymns.

Havergal and her father are buried near each other at Astley Church. The inscription on Frances' tomb reads: "By her writings in prose and verse she being dead yet speaketh." These words touched me deeply, reminding me how our influence goes on long after we die, something we don't always think about when we're alive.

Our tour leader, an organist and pianist, led our group in several choruses of the beautiful hymn that is a testimony to the life of Frances Havergal. To this day the lyrics she wrote are a call to everyone who wants to live for Christ alone.

> Take my life, and let it be
> Consecrated, Lord, to Thee;
> Take my moments and my days—
> Let them flow in ceaseless praise.
> Let them flow in ceaseless praise.

As the tour bus left this inspiring site, I realized that this visit, the history I was learning, and the opportunity to sing these great hymns in the very places where they were composed were enriching and rekindling my relationship with God in ways I hadn't imagined. I felt like a bride, happy and excited about what was to come. I also knew in my heart that opening a new chapter in my relationship with God didn't mean working hard at prayer and service.

Rather, like Frances, all I had to do was dedicate every day to the Lord and let each moment be a ceaseless flow of praise by the thoughts I have, the work I do, and the emotions that come over me.

From Sheep Farmer to Hymn Composer

After a hearty breakfast one morning later that week we drove the short distance to Wales with a planned stop at Llandovery to visit the Welsh farmhouse that had been the home of William Williams, the "sweet singer of Wales," as people referred to him. Grazing sheep, rolling hills, and a blanket of blue sky greeted us this day, reminiscent of the landscape Williams himself enjoyed most days of his life (1717–1791).

The current owners of the estate are his sixth-generation relatives. They have dedicated one of the rooms to his memory, featuring a variety of Williams' writings, photographs, and memorabilia. After a brief lecture, we moved to the small living room, still featuring the composer's desk in a corner by a window. We took our songbooks in hand and sang the hymn that Williams is perhaps best known for, "Guide Me, O Thou Great Jehovah," giving thanks for this great man whose life and writings still inspire Christians around the world.

> Guide Me, O Thou great Jehovah,
> Pilgrim through this barren land.
> I am weak, but Thou art mighty;
> Hold me with Thy powerful hand.
> Bread of Heaven, Bread of Heaven,
> Feed me till I want no more;
> Feed me till I want no more.

The lyrics of this hymn really spoke to me. I had spent so much of my life striving under my own misguided power that I had neglected to ask God to hold me and feed me by his powerful hand.

In addition to his devotion to Christ and his burning desire to put his thoughts to music, William Williams became an influential and powerful preacher. He had a gift for assessing people's religious maturity and experience, which helped him minister effectively to the men and women he met all over the Welsh countryside. The author of more than 90 volumes and pamphlets on various topics and extensive poetry, he is considered the nation's greatest literary figure of the eighteenth century.

The Desire to Know God

Throughout history, people of every nationality and background long for divine guidance, regardless of their religious practices and beliefs. Our desire to know God never really disappears. "Guide Me, O Thou Great Jehovah" reminds us of that longing that is at the depth of every heart, even today, decades after it was written.

I often think of that special afternoon in the Williams cottage, and I could weep all over again. The humble and simple words of this particular hymn brought me down to where I ought to be— submitted to God in every thought, word, and deed. Like so many well-meaning followers of Christ, I thought that drawing nearer to God meant *doing* more instead of simply *being*.

Cheddar Gorge

Another memorable experience on our musical tour was a stop outside Cheddar Gorge, named as the second greatest natural wonder in Britain. A long vertical cleft in a mighty rock nearby boasts a sign that announces to tourists the place where composer Augustus Toplady (1740–1778) found shelter during a frightening storm. Legend has it he wrote the inspiring "Rock of Ages," one of the most-beloved Christian hymns, shortly after his experience of being stranded. I stood in the cleft as my husband took several photos. *Am I really here?* I asked myself as I stood in the cleft where Augustus Toplady stood so many ages ago. I shivered at the thought. What a privilege!

Rock of Ages, cleft for me,
Let me hide myself in Thee;
Let the water and the blood,
From Thy wounded side which flowed,
Be of sin the double cure;
Save from wrath and make me pure.

A sermon delivered in a barn in Ireland in 1755 had brought Toplady to Christ. Many people considered him a loner but still a spiritual preacher as the vicar of St. Andrew's Church in Broadhembury. Although Toplady wrote 130 hymns in total, "Rock of Ages" is the one millions of people the world over love and sing to this day. The words seem to cry out mankind's deepest desire—to be hidden in Christ. It is certainly my desire, especially as I grow older.

Grace Amazing

John Newton (1725–1807), a former slave trader, wrote the most popular hymn of all time, "Amazing Grace." After many years of living a life he later regretted, he became the curate and preacher of the Church of St. Peter and St. Paul in Olney, a market town in the Borough of Milton Keynes, South East England, from 1764–1780. Our group was able to learn about Newton's journey as well—from slave trader to follower of Christ.

Amazing Grace! How sweet the sound
That saved a wretch like me!
I once was lost, but now am found;
Was blind, but now I see.

'Twas Grace that taught my heart to fear,
And Grace my fears relieved.
How precious did that Grace appear
The hour I first believed.

Although Newton's mother had taught him Bible lessons and the hymns of Isaac Watts when Newton was very young, she died when he was just six years old. Without her influence, he grew away from the faith and began sailing with his father. Over the years he served on a naval ship and then joined the crew of a slave ship. In March 1748, a fierce storm threatened his life and those of his shipmates. Newton prayed for the first time in years and committed his life to Christ.

Transformed by Faith

I was encouraged so much to read about these amazing saints and to study and sing the words of their hymns. They, too, struggled with life. They, too, faced their own egos and arrogance. And like us, they, too, realized they could not make it through this life without bowing to the God who loves them with an everlasting love and unconditional forgiveness.

Our wondrous trip ended several days later, but the memories I made are with me still. I returned home transformed in my Christian faith by the lyrics of these beautiful hymns and the lives of the composers who traveled the road long before I was born. I'm so grateful to them and for them and for my renewed friendship with God.

Many Ways to Be Refreshed

Not everyone can travel across the world to visit such places in person, but the stories and hymns and history of the past related to our God can build up our faith and foster new insights.

I've tried no less than four times to go to Israel, and for some reason or another it has never worked out. Finally, I accepted the fact that I'm not going to get there. So I read a book on Israel written by a friend who beautifully documented her trip, and I watched a DVD tour of Israel led by Pastor Jack Hayford. Now I'm satisfied. Sometimes we have to accept what is and find a way to receive the benefits of something we want by another means. God can speak to us in ways we don't expect.

When you get into a trouble spot or you feel down and out for any reason, consider listening to or, even better, singing one or more of these hymns and meditating on the awesome words. God is with us, and he will heal our hearts and dry our tears as we accept the challenge of deepening our faith through prayer, worship, praise, and learning from these great Christian men and women who have taken the lead.

. . . .

Wit:

"Always have something beautiful in sight, even if it's just a daisy in a jelly glass." H. Jackson Brown Jr.

Wisdom:

"He put a new song in my mouth, a hymn of praise to our God" (Psalm 40:3).

Willpower:

"Today I will pray in song even if I sing out of tune."

26

The Power of Breath

Opening a New Chapter on Wellness

"Catch your breath."

"Just breathe."

"I'm out of breath."

"I can't breathe."

"Relax. Take a deep breath."

We've all heard or said these popular phrases about breathing. When in shock or fear, it's always helpful to take a breath. To sleep soundly, deep-breathing exercises can help us drift off. When we're walking, or swimming, or hiking, or bike riding, our breathing escalates and we become more aware of it. But most of our lives we just breathe—because that's what we do to function and to stay alive. We may think about the benefits of deep breathing to relax, to refresh ourselves, to cleanse our organs, but we often don't follow through, especially as we mature.

During our golden years, our breathing can become ragged, shallow, and difficult due to illness and just plain habit. We get used to a certain pattern, and we live with it. For a more cheerful disposition, however, and a surge in energy, consider the benefits of deep breathing a few times a day.

7 Habits of Highly Successful Breathers

1. *Improve your supply of oxygen.* You fill up your car with fuel. How about filling up your lungs with the fuel of oxygen? Your life depends on it, and so does your blood. Imagine the illnesses you may prevent by simply breathing well and deeply.

2. *Relax your nerves.* You've probably heard people say, "I'm a nervous wreck," or "You're getting on my nerves." Did you know that one of the best ways to take care of your nerves is to *breathe* consciously and deliberately? What a difference it can make in just a moment or two! You can nourish your nervous system (the spinal cord, nerves, and brain) with just a couple of cleansing breaths, and they will also help you *think* more clearly.

3. *Calm your muscles.* Instead of popping a pill, pop a breath and feel your muscles relax after a good workout, or a stressful day babysitting grandchildren, or tending to a sick mate. You'll feel energized instead of depleted, and you'll have a reserve for the next day.

4. *Control blood pressure.* Many of us goldens find our blood pressure goes up the older we get, and we have to take medication to bring it under control. But some people are finding alternatives to drugs, and one of them is to take long deep breaths periodically throughout the day as well as exercising and using other natural remedies. Recently, I've been able to give up my medications through these methods.

5. *Be good to your lungs and heart.* The best way to care for your heart is to reduce its workload and, at the same time, help

your lungs operate more efficiently. The more effectively the heart and lungs carry out their duties, the healthier and more alive you'll feel.

6. *Enhance your emotional health.* When you breathe evenly, deeply, and regularly, you may notice you are less easily overwhelmed with everyday matters, petty squabbles, and irritations from others, as well as depressive thoughts and worries. Deep breaths seem to clear our minds so we can see a situation for what it is and respond appropriately rather than overreact negatively.

7. *Deepen your spiritual life.* You may wonder what breathing has to do with prayer and meditation. A lot. We can't concentrate on speaking and listening to God unless we slow down and focus. During a busy day it takes a deliberate act on our part to do just that. Stopping to close our eyes and take some deep breaths will bring us into a setting and posture of mind and spirit that allows us to commune with God in an intimate and deeply satisfying way.

Abdominal Breathing Technique

Here's an exercise that helps me every night now that I've tried it and had success. It's especially useful whenever I'm experiencing upsetting thoughts, pain, or stress—day or night.

- Place one hand on your chest and the other on your abdomen. Take a deep breath in, making sure the hand on the abdomen rises higher than the one on the chest to ensure the diaphragm is pulling air into the bottom of your lungs.

- Exhale through your mouth and then breathe in slowly through your nose, pretending you're taking in all the air in the room. Hold it for a count of five to seven, no higher.

- Slowly exhale through your mouth for a count of eight. As the air releases, gently contract your abdominal muscles to completely evacuate the remaining air. We deepen respirations not by inhaling more air but by exhaling it completely.

- Repeat the cycle three or four more times for a total of five deep breaths. Try to breathe at a rate of one breath every ten seconds. You'll notice your heart rate increase, producing a positive effect on cardiac health.

Some people consider such techniques nonsense. They'd rather sip a glass of wine or stay up so late at night they literally fall into bed exhausted. Neither one is effective in the long run and may result in alcohol dependency, chronic fatigue, depression, or all three. If you're willing to give this breathing technique an honest try, you might be surprised at how effective it is.

Why not also try incorporating short prayers to enhance the exercise? For example with each inhalation: "Come, Holy Spirit, and help me calm down." And with each exhalation: "Thank you for the courage to keep going." The idea is to invite God's Spirit to be with you as you inhale. Then, as you exhale, release the troubling thought or action and focus on God's love and grace.

. . . .

Wit:

"When you arise in the morning, think of what a precious privilege it is to be alive." MARCUS AURELIUS

Wisdom:

"The Spirit of God has made me; the breath of the Almighty gives me life" (Job 33:4).

Willpower:

"Today I will arise and breathe in the breath of God to think, to enjoy, to love."

27

Taking It Easy

Opening a New Chapter on Slowing Down

Sooner or later we all have to slow down—whether we feel like it or not. Physical age takes over, and we don't have a choice. We can't tie our shoes without sitting down first. We can't catch up with our grandchildren running a block ahead of us. And a nap sounds mighty delicious now and again. Let's face it. We're getting older, and gravity is taking its toll.

Some of us dread it. We can't accept it. We won't admit it. Others go with the flow. They embrace it. And still others take a deep breath and simply endure it. Some weeks ago I rediscovered the *up*side of slowing down. I gave in to the peace and joy, rest and simplicity, and the warmth and relaxation of simply taking it easy—a very new experience for me.

Saying No and Meaning It

I looked at my calendar one recent weekend and saw I had booked myself up and down from morning till late afternoon on both Saturday and Sunday. My stomach churned as I imagined doing all the things I had lined up. How could I have done this to myself *again*? I didn't have an answer except to realize that if there was even a small space open, I tended to fill it. I thought about that for a while and let it soak in.

For Saturday I'd said yes to an open house and luncheon sponsored by our local symphony. I knew I wanted to do that, but I also wanted to spend the day weeding my garden, buying some new pots, tearing out the dead blossoms, and planting summer flowers in their place.

And on Sunday church was in the morning, a memorial service on the other side of town in the afternoon, and a worship celebration at church that night. My laundry had piled up, and I could see a layer of dust on my living room furniture. I let out a sigh and dropped into a nearby chair. *Something has to give*, I chided myself, *or you're going to give out.* I couldn't argue. My *self* was right. Only I could change the pattern here and set the weekend a-right.

I wrestled with the part of me that wants to please others by showing up when I'm invited, participating in events whether or not I'm interested or have the energy, and feeling I owe it to myself and others to keep going no matter what. Or was I, perhaps, turning into a FOMO (a person who has a Fear of Missing Out).

I stopped long enough to look at my list and cross off what I didn't really want to do. I didn't want to attend the memorial—too much driving on a busy highway on a Sunday afternoon. I didn't want to go to evening worship. I'd just been to the regular early service. I also didn't feel like dusting and vacuuming.

What did I *want* to do? Attend the symphony luncheon and recital and purchase flowers and plant them—and then take an afternoon nap. So that's what I did, and I felt jubilant about it! My entire week was better for having slowed down on the weekend and doing only what I really *wanted* to do and what I had the energy to do.

Slowing down doesn't come easily. Sometimes illness, a broken relationship, a job loss, financial collapse, a wayward child, or a difficult relative might force us to stop and take an inventory of our lives. What is God saying to us at such a time? He may be asking us to remember that he is God, he is Lord, he is the only one who can restore a broken heart, comfort us through a numbing loss, and clarify a confusing experience. And he will do all of these things and more if we slow down long enough to hear his voice and to take up activities that turn our hearts toward him. When we follow this path, we are more likely to find ourselves laughing all the way.

. . . .

Wit:

"All you need is love. But a little chocolate now and then doesn't hurt." CHARLES SCHULTZ

Wisdom:

"Be still, and know that I am God" (Psalm 46:10).

Willpower:

"Today I will take time to slow down—to observe, to think, to *be*."

28

Simple Simplicity

Opening a New Chapter to Less Clutter

I remember a time years ago when I decided to clear out the clutter in my apartment and simplify my life. I didn't need 100 books, 3 sets of dishes, 102 paintings and plaques on the walls, and clothes I rarely wore. So out, out, out! I was going to start fresh. It felt good just to think about it.

"Simplicity," says Richard Foster, "sets us free to receive the provision of God as a gift that is not ours to keep, and that can be freely shared with others."

Those words spoke to me when I first read them 35 years ago, and they still do today. Simplicity means taking our hands off the controls and depending on God, as do the birds of the air and the lilies of the field (Matthew 6:26-29 AMPC). Making a decision to simplify and putting it into practice, however, is not that simple. It requires trust, first of all, followed by prudent decisions. I knew I had some work to do. I had to accept the challenge of living a simpler, more streamlined life, including clothing, my car, and even groceries.

Do we really need fourteen pairs of shoes, six sweaters, and ten bill caps? Can we live in a modest dwelling that fits our needs and is affordable rather than a showplace that drains our savings? Simplicity also encourages us to modify our diets and to enjoy simple, nourishing foods we can prepare at home and share with neighbors and friends instead of relying on fast-food stops and expensive restaurants.

What About Mother Earth?

The simple life also challenges us to be concerned about our planet and its resources. If you eat meat, how about experimenting with a few vegetarian meals each week? You could give up paper goods and choose cloth wipes that can be reused. As you walk in your neighborhood or along the shore, pick up the bits of trash you see. I often keep a plastic bag in my pocket for such items. This doesn't mean we have to be a major trash collector, but when we see a stray candy wrapper or some small windblown item in our path, we pick it up and dispose of it in the nearest container. It might sound rather silly, or we might prefer to leave it to the city to clean it up, but every bit of help we can offer is another step toward living a richer, simpler life.

Unloading Paper Clutter

My dad collected copies of *Time* magazine—to the point that they took up half the space in my parents' spare closet. Mom used to smuggle small stacks out of the house when Dad wasn't looking. He didn't miss them because he never reread any of the issues. Collecting had become a habit. He felt certain he'd look through them again someday. He never did.

A few years ago I decided to drop my newspaper and magazine

subscriptions. Now I'm free of those bills and of the paper clutter they added to my house. I visit the library where I can browse the issues I'm interested in and then leave them behind for someone else. How liberating to use something without owning it! Imagine how lovely it would be to let go of dusting, fixing, and replacing items that break or wear out. Such freedom!

Simplifying Emotional Clutter

One aspect of the simple life we sometimes overlook is our tie to circumstances, traditions, outdated belief systems, and habits. We hang on to people who no longer nourish us, to ideals that no longer support our lives, and to customs we've outgrown.

- Who says we *have* to decorate a Christmas tree every year? What if we would be just as happy with a few small holiday ornaments and candles placed here and there that can be put up and taken down in ten minutes or less?

- Who says we have to prepare a major Thanksgiving dinner for a family of 30 when we don't feel up to it anymore?

- Who says we have to continue playing bridge every Friday afternoon when we'd rather take a walk or a nap?

Can we *accept* what it will take to simplify our lives? At first it will take some work, some letting go, and some new ways of looking at our routines and what really matters to us during these golden years.

Inner Simplicity

Perhaps most important of all is simplifying our life in the spiritual sense. For example, could we talk less and listen to God more? Could we wait on the Lord more, and hurry less? Could we rely on the wisdom of the Holy Spirit more and less on our own "good" ideas?

Simplicity is not the same thing as austerity. Austerity renounces the things of this world; simplicity puts things in proper perspective. Simplicity encourages us to be well, look well, feel well, and do well without making a show of it. Simplicity allows us to drive an older car because we want to, not because we have to. Or to drive a new car for the same reason. Like the apostle Paul, we can be content in plenty or in want (see Philippians 4:11-13). We can accept the challenge of doing with less so we can be more on target for God. Simplicity begins within. When we are simple on the inside, we are free on the outside.

· · · · · · · · · · ·

Wit:

"We never repent of having eaten too little." THOMAS JEFFERSON

Wisdom:

"Do not worry, saying, 'What shall we eat?' or 'What shall we drink?' or 'What shall we wear?'... Seek first his kingdom and his righteousness, and all these things will be given to you" (Matthew 6:31,33).

Willpower:

"Today I will look at ways to simplify my life and then take a step forward."

29

As Good as Your Word

Opening a New Chapter on Honesty

I answered on the first ring.

"Hi, Karen. I've been putting off this call for a while. But today I have the courage to pick up the phone."

My stomach churned. I knew the voice. Beth. One of my book-club friends. In that moment I wished I had caller ID. I would have ignored this one. On the other hand, I had to deal with the problem between us. Might as well bite the bullet and get through it.

I paused and took a breath. "What's up?"

"You know good and well." Her voice simmered. "I thought we were friends."

"I thought so too." But did I really? Beth had been a sore spot for months now, always wanting more from me than I wanted to give. She was divorced and lonely, and I found her controlling. My head was filled with her unsolicited advice.

"I've brought you homemade soup when you were sick, a book I knew you'd love for Christmas, and that knitted scarf, remember? I went to five stores to find the perfect one, by the way."

"Very thoughtful of you." I could barely get the words out.

"Is that all you can say? You sent me a birthday card and that was that."

I took another breath. It was time to say what I meant without being mean. "Beth, I do consider you a friend. I have enjoyed our conversations, and I like knowing we both love reading good books. But beyond that, I don't know what to say. I have a lot of people in my life, and I don't make a habit of giving gifts to everyone. It's too much to keep track of and, frankly, too expensive. I hope my presence and my support are expressions of my friendship."

I could hear Beth breathing. I knew I had to let the truth stand.

"Beth, please hear me. I care about you and I wish the best for you—always—but you seem to want more from me than I'm able to give. I'm sorry if that's disappointing to hear, but I can't pretend and I'm not going to lie."

The silence between us rose up like a wall. For once I did not tear it down with words. I let it stand. Finally, Beth muttered a weak, "If that's the way you want to be..."

"Thank you for calling," I said. "I'll see you at the next book-club meeting."

Except I didn't. She left the group, and I didn't see her again for a couple of years. Sometime later I received a note asking me if we could reconnect. She felt bad about how our relationship had ended. I thought about it but knew I couldn't go back. I told her I wasn't ready for that and wished her well.

A Path Well Worn

That may sound mean spirited on my part, but I saw it as being true to my word and to my feelings. No good can come from pretense. I'd been down that path too many times in my life.

Above all, my brothers and sisters, do not swear—not by
heaven or by earth or by anything else. All you need to say
is a simple "Yes" or "No." Otherwise you will be condemned.
                                                          JAMES 5:12

I've often wondered why it has been difficult for me to say yes or no. To speak my truth, to face an obstacle such as a strong-willed person like Beth. Maybe because avoidance lets me off the hook in the moment or relieves me from having to follow through? Or maybe I'm just stunned when someone is forceful with me? Maybe I can't face the truth long enough to express it out loud?

No matter the reason, God expects us to be honest and clear in our communication so we won't be condemned by our own words. Oh, how many times I have experienced my own condemnation just because I was afraid or unwilling to speak honestly and openly when I had the opportunity.

I recall a time when a new neighbor came to my door in the apartment building where I lived at the time. I was about to dish up the pasta I had prepared for dinner when I heard a knock.

I opened the door. "Got a minute?" asked the woman standing before me.

"Sure," I lied. "No problem." I invited her in, all the while thinking about my dinner going cold on the stove.

She stuck out her hand. "Hi, Karen. I'm Linda. I just moved into 3-C. I'm having a game night next Friday, and I'd love you to come. Since I'm new in the building I figured the best way to meet people is to throw a party. It would be a great chance to get better acquainted."

My mind took over, ignoring my heart. I wanted to say yes so she wouldn't be disappointed. At the same time I wanted to say no so I wouldn't put myself in a predicament. I knew I couldn't make it—didn't want to make it. I don't particularly care for table games, and I keep Friday nights open to rest and watch TV or read and pamper myself after a long workweek.

Then I thought of a third option—tell her I'll call her after I check my calendar. Still another idea occurred to me. Say yes and see how it goes. I could always call and cancel the day before. I'd find a reasonable excuse.

Lies, lies, and more lies. Why couldn't I just tell the truth in the moment? I could be kind, of course, but still be honest.

Facing Myself

I felt the Holy Spirit's nudge. I thanked Linda for the invitation and then told her Friday nights were my date nights with myself. She laughed. "I should do something like that," she said. "What a good idea. Well, I'll see you by the pool, and maybe we can talk then."

I agreed. We parted on good terms, and I felt happy with myself. As I look back on my life, I see many other such nooks and crannies where the dust collects, where I cut corners, where I close my eyes to the lies.

But a life of spiritual integrity demands more than merely getting by. It requires that I be true to my word, and, more importantly, to God's Word. When we say what we mean "without saying it mean," as the slogan goes, we honor the Lord, show respect for others, and lay a foundation of accountability in our lives that keeps us faithful to the truth regardless of the circumstances.

We've all been known to speak without making a point, or to toss words into the air for no reason, or to fill up space with chitchat, even to back away from conversations where the truth could make a difference in the life of another person. By speaking my truth to

Linda, she admitted she could use a date night with herself too. So in a way, my admission was a gift to her.

God's grace and courage will help us make a fresh start. Realizing we are only as good as our word, we're more likely to be thoughtful about the words we choose—and use.

. . . .

Wit:

"Honesty is the rarest wealth anyone can possess, and yet all the honesty in the world ain't lawful tender for a loaf of bread." JOSH BILLINGS

Wisdom:

"We are taking pains to do what is right, not only in the eyes of the Lord but also in the eyes of man" (2 Corinthians 8:21).

Willpower:

"Today I will say what I mean without saying it mean."

30

Ah! Sweet Sleep

Opening a New Chapter on Rest

"Mom, what are you doing up at this hour?" I heard my mother tip-toeing past my room at 3:00 one early morning. The door squeaked as she pulled it closed so as not to disturb my sister and me.

"I can't sleep," she said, sighing. "I'm headed downstairs for a glass of milk. I'm also going to try to walk off this restlessness in my legs."

I was a teenager at the time, and I sure hoped I wouldn't be walking the house in the middle of the night when I was her age. I enjoyed a good night's sleep most of my young life. But sure enough, when I hit menopause all bets were off. I was up and down several times a night to use the bathroom and then stared at the stars for a moment or two before going back to bed. It seemed I'd never get a full night's sleep again.

I knew, as we all do, that sleep is essential for a person's health and well-being, a fact many of us ignore according to the National Sleep Foundation. But we can't force ourselves to sleep. I learned I wasn't alone. There are plenty of people pacing in the dark or tossing and turning when they should be resting their bones.

Pills or Prayers?

For a while I relied on over-the-counter natural sleep aids, but before long they didn't help. I was back to where I'd started, frustrated and confused about what to do. I heard that sleeplessness was a symptom of aging, but I was certain I was too young to accept that verdict. And I didn't find anything to laugh about in this predicament.

So I did a bit of research online and found many suggestions, including practicing breathing exercises, taking daily walks, drinking plenty of water, eating a healthy diet, focusing on positive thoughts, avoiding electronics before bed, listening to music, wearing a sleep mask to darken surroundings, tracking fears and setting them aside, all of which can contribute to peaceful sleep.

A Good Night's Sleep at Last

For me, however, the most important solution I discovered is a spiritual one—and I found it in Scripture.

> *When you lie down, you will not be afraid; when you lie down, your sleep will be sweet.*
>
> PROVERBS 3:24

I have made this verse a regular nightly prayer. And when worry about my children, my writing career, household bills, health issues, or the state of our world poke my mind at night, I remember the power I have to change my thinking. I turn to prayers instead of pills.

> *We demolish arguments and every pretension that sets itself up against the knowledge of God, and we take captive every thought to make it obedient to Christ.*
>
> 2 CORINTHIANS 10:5

I now see that the best sleep medicine is God's Word! I practice it in my own life, and I encourage you with the following suggestions as you climb into bed each night.

- Browse verses from the Bible that will quiet your mind and soothe your soul. "Your hand will guide me, your right hand will hold me fast" (Psalm 139:10). "The LORD watches over you—the LORD is your shade at your right hand" (Psalm 121:5).

- Read a brief meditation or devotion from a trusted author. I recommend *My Utmost for His Highest* by Oswald Chambers and *Morning and Evening* by Charles Spurgeon.

- Breathe deeply, inhaling and exhaling slowly for five minutes.

- Listen to a CD featuring worship songs or relaxation music.

If you need additional help, contact a certified therapist or spiritual leader with whom you can talk over your problems to find solutions to the situations that are interrupting your sleep.

As Christians we have the privilege and the opportunity *by the Lord's invitation* to cast our cares on him instead of keeping them under wraps (see 1 Peter 5:7.) Worry and fear exhaust us as we face and deal with our daily challenges. When we call on God, we can lay our head on the pillow at night trusting that our sleep will indeed be sweet. And the next morning, we may find ourselves smiling instead of yawning or rubbing our eyes, looking forward to a day of discovery and laughter.

Wit:

"In the morning you beg to sleep more, in the afternoon you are dying to sleep, and at night you refuse to sleep." AUTHOR UNKNOWN

Wisdom:

"When you lie down, you will not be afraid; when you lie down, your sleep will be sweet" (Proverbs 3:24).

Willpower:

"Tonight I will count my blessings instead of sheep."

31

Peace-Filled Living

Opening a New Chapter on Contentment

"Karen." My dad tapped my hand. "Stop nibbling your fingernails." He also caught my attention with a stern look when I twirled and cartwheeled across the living-room floor. I was a busy, high-strung child, apparently too active for him. As I grew older I settled down, afraid to be too noisy, too showy, too much.

By the time I reached my teens, I was a shadow of my former self—fearful, anxious, and lacking self-confidence. I don't blame my father for the change. He was simply trying to calm me down in a household of three kids, a dog, and my grandfather in our tiny two-bedroom house.

College life offered me new opportunities away from home and the watchful eyes of my parents. I welcomed each experience. I received above-average grades, appeared in school plays, and even attracted a boyfriend. Still, I felt discontentment. Something was missing, but I couldn't put my finger on it.

Two weeks after graduation, I married my sweetheart and moved from Illinois to California, which felt like another world. Within five years I was a mother to three children and the wife of a man who spent most of his hours working or studying toward a degree in law. I felt alone and restless, even though my son and two daughters brought me many joyful hours. I continued to live on this plane until the year I turned 41—the year I met Jesus Christ following a painful divorce and a health crisis.

At the urging of a friend, I purchased my first Bible and enrolled in a Scripture study, unaware that it was the beginning of my personal journey toward contentment. My teachers and companions on this path were writers who lived hundreds of years before I was born, but their wisdom on the Gospels (Matthew, Mark, Luke, John) and Psalms and letters to Christ followers led the way, and they are with me still.

The road to contentment is different for each person. I'm still traveling mine. Here are a few of the verses that spoke to me along the way.

John 14:6

"I am the way and the truth and the life. No one comes to the Father except through me."

This was the first verse to capture my heart as I studied the Gospel according to John with a group of women at a local church. I leaned in to every word and listened to others share their experience of knowing Jesus Christ in a deeply personal way. This possibility was absolutely news to me.

Days later after a jog along the beach near my home, I stopped on a bench overlooking the ocean and cried out to God. "Lord, I'm yours. I confess my sins and ask you to lead me from now on." I walked home a new woman in Christ, just as the Bible promises. (See 2 Corinthians 5:17.) I took a deep breath, suddenly free of the worry and fear about my future. I knew I no longer had to carry my burdens alone.

Romans 8:1

"There is now no condemnation for those who are in Christ Jesus."

What good news! For years I had carried the weight of my sin—confessing, feeling guilty, asking for forgiveness, and then falling again. I seemed as helpless as Paul claimed to be when he wrote to the Romans about himself: "I have the desire to do what is good, but I cannot carry it out. For I do not do the good I want to do, but the evil I do not want to do—this I keep on doing" (Romans 7:18-19).

After I took to heart that in Christ there is no condemnation because I am loved unconditionally, I took God at his word, as Paul did. "Thanks be to God, who delivers me through Jesus Christ our Lord!" (Romans 7:25). I am now guilt-free and safe in Christ.

John 10:10

"I [Jesus] have come that they may have life, and have it to the full."

One morning years ago I tried to figure out what this verse really means, since my life had certainly not been a garden of flowers. What did it mean that God's purpose was to give me life to the full? I mulled the words around for a while and then suddenly an insight dropped into my mind. I felt God impressing on me what I needed to hear. It struck me that a *full* life is one that has a variety of experiences, among them joy, sorrow, pain, healing, challenge, and victory.

Today when I read these words, I'm filled with peace, knowing that God has a *full* life for each of his sons and daughters, so I shouldn't be surprised or disappointed with any of it. I'll be challenged, but I'll never be alone. God will be with me through each experience, teaching me what I need to know and leading me on the right path.

As I write this, I'm looking at that verse in a frame on my desk—a gift from a friend. I read it several times a week, especially when difficulties invade my peace.

Proverbs 3:5

"Trust in the LORD *with all your heart and lean not on your own understanding."*

This verse has seen me through many anxious moments, such as when my daughter moved to Africa for a season, when my son lived apart from our family for two years, when my husband lost his job without warning, when my mother had a stroke and lost her ability to speak, and when a book I'd written was suddenly cancelled right before publication. I hung on to these words, putting my hope in the Lord and not in doctors, or publishers, or employers. I couldn't control illnesses, jobs, the results of my writing, or my children's choices. But God promised he'd be present in all these situations and bring them together for the good of each of us.

Psalm 126:5

"Those who sow with tears will reap with songs of joy."

I found special comfort in these words as I thought about my past—the shame I experienced when I had to ask for rent money from the church Deacon's Fund one month when my husband and I were flat broke and the heartache I felt as I watched my father die right before my eyes. I knew in the deepest part of me that God was there and that my tears would one day turn to joy. I also knew it was going to take time—and that was okay. I could be content no matter what.

Isaiah 46:4

"Even to your old age and gray hairs I am he, I am he who will sustain you. I have made you and I will carry you; I will sustain you and I will rescue you."

Today I'm an older woman with gray hair (mostly white). I know with certainty that God is still with me, holding on to me and keeping me close. I am his beloved, as is each one of us. He made me and he will sustain me and even carry me when harm threatens.

My journey toward contentment is ongoing, step-by-deliberate-step, sometimes slow, sometimes fast, with plenty of pauses along the way for conversations with God, for praise and prayer, for smiles and tears, but always with a deep knowing that I am not alone, never have been, and never will be as long as I stay close to God through Jesus Christ.

Today I know that my Redeemer lives—and he lives in me. I am more than content. And that contentment is possible for you too. Seize it and smile.

. . . .

Wit:

"You know you are getting old when the candles on your birthday cake start to cost more than the cake itself." AUTHOR UNKNOWN

Wisdom:

"I have learned the secret of being content in any and every situation, whether well fed or hungry, whether living in plenty or in want" (Philippians 4:12).

Willpower:

"Today I will get out of bed and rejoice that I am still alive. I will be content exactly where I am."

32

A Privilege Few Experience

Opening a New Chapter to the Golden Years

The day I turned 65 I was excited (Social Security checks!) and deflated over the reality that I was growing old and there was no turning back. But not long after that birthday I gained an entirely new perspective on this thing called aging. One hot summer day, my husband and I drove the high-and-winding road to the top of the White Mountains in California. When we arrived at the ranger station situated at 12,000 feet, we gasped for breath in the thin, chilly air. I grabbed a parka and wool cap, and minutes later, with map in hand, we set off on the four-mile trail that led through a forest of ancient pines, where some of the oldest trees on the planet were still thriving. We were in search of the oldest, dubbed "Methuselah." We found out, however, that its exact location is a secret so visitors will not take samples. We had fun guessing which one it was.

At the end of our hike, we made a 12-mile drive to the Patriarch Forest, where more ancient trees crowded together in the midst of a barren piece of land where no human life existed. The unpaved road was rock-strewn and bumpy, and the air was hot and thick with dust.

I felt like a pioneer in a covered wagon, though our station wagon had air-conditioning.

Twelve miles on such a road can ruin the tires and break down the motor. My pulse took off. The afternoon sun was already tilting to the west, and I feared we might get stuck on the side of the road with no help available. Would AAA come this far to rescue us? I shuddered, imagining the worst.

I didn't want to turn back too soon, though. I knew this would be our first and last trip to the White Mountains. We pressed on, and finally I spotted a small sign that led to a parking lot beside the grove.

I jumped out of the car, eager to hug a tree and grateful we'd made it. We walked the trail, stopping here and there to comment on the shape, or color, or texture of these amazing specimens that had been on this soil thousands of years before Jesus was born. To me it was holy ground. I wanted to congratulate each tree for surviving, for being steadfast, for doing what God had created it to do. Standing in this wilderness for thousands of years was proof enough to me that they had what it takes to stay alive and thrive.

Every one of these trees showed their age and more. There was no hiding their humps, bumps, gnarled branches, and chubby trunks. They were anything but beautiful when compared with a graceful willow, yet I found them lovely in their own way. The ravages of age and weather had bestowed an elegance I couldn't describe.

I thought about myself, an older woman with a few humps and bumps of my own. I'd been hard on myself, I realized, finding fault with my looks and the toll the aging process had taken. How could I see beauty in the trees but not in me? Why is getting older a good thing for a tree but a bad thing for me? Why do I look in the mirror and bemoan the wrinkles that line my face, but see in the trees a quiet dignity that has nothing to do with shape or age? I had a good cry as the truth of these words and feelings sank in.

My husband and I drove back in silence, each one wrapped in our own thoughts. What had begun as an exciting adventure turned into a personal retreat. Colorful conversation gave way to quiet reflection.

Lord, how ungrateful of me to judge my worth by what I see. I know that I am more to you than a lump of aging clay. Thank you for the gifts of wisdom and discernment, for curiosity, for peace, and for your ever-lasting love. Amen.

Today I am an old woman, pushing into my 80s. I thank God for the opportunity to have lived this long and to continue to con-tribute with the gifts I've been given. I really do see that getting old is a privilege few people get to enjoy and appreciate. As we become more aware of this privilege, we're more likely to finish out our lives laughing all the way—with gratitude and joy.

* * * * * * * * * * *

Wit:

"I don't know how to act my age because I've never been this old before." AUTHOR UNKNOWN

Wisdom:

"The beginning of wisdom is this: Get wisdom. Though it cost all you have, get understanding" (Isaiah 46:4).

Willpower:

"Today I will thank God for the gift of age and the grace to sus-tain it."

About the Author

Karen O'Connor has authored many magazine articles and more than 70 books, including *Walkin' with God Ain't for Wimps* and *Gettin' Old Ain't for Wimps* (more than 300,000 copies sold). Her numerous awards include the Paul A. Witty Award for short story writing and the 2002 Special Recognition Award at the Mount Hermon Christian Writers Conference.

Karen inspires her readers with hope, help, and plenty of humor, encouraging them to:

- experience and express more joy and gratitude
- achieve greater intimacy with God, self, and others
- polish communication and leadership skills

Karen speaks at schools, churches, and community organizations, and she has been a guest on national radio and television programs, including *Faith at Work, Coast-to-Coast, Lifestyle Magazine,* and *The 700 Club.*

Karen loves to connect with her readers. Find out more about her at www.karenoconnor.com.

If you enjoyed reading Laughing All the Way,
you'll also get a kick out of...

Humor Is the New Fountain of Youth

If you're thirsty for a good chuckle, drink up! Stay forever young with these whimsical, slice-of-senior-life stories from bestselling humorist Karen O' Connor. These amusing anecdotes on aging celebrate the hilarious highs and laugh-out-loud lows that can only come from decades of experience. Maybe you'll see a little bit of yourself as you encounter

- medication mix-ups
- code cracking chaos
- diet dos-and-don'ts
- vexing vocabulary
- wardrobe worries

Along with all the fun comes a fresh dose of inspiration from Scripture and a short prayer to help you reflect on the things that truly matter—faith, family, and friendship.

Kick back, relax, and enjoy this heartfelt collection of golden years glimpses that are sure to bring a smile to your face.

More Great Books by Karen O'Connor!

With humor and wisdom, speaker and author Karen O'Connor urges fellow baby boomers to celebrate every moment. Personal and gathered stories capture the trials and joys faced when one survives and surpasses middle-age.

O'Connor's delightful storytelling resounds in these short vignettes based on real life. You'll chuckle as you read these funny, heartwarming experiences and then share them with your friends. Each humorous tale concludes with a biblical principle to encourage you in your spiritual walk and an uplifting prayer.

To learn more about Harvest House books and
to read sample chapters, visit our website:

www.harvesthousepublishers.com

HARVEST HOUSE PUBLISHERS
EUGENE, OREGON